DOORS:
Where Hope Resides

DOORS:
Where Hope Resides

LINDA WIMES
Bestselling Author of *You Have to be Willing to Die*

Doors: Where Hope Resides

Copyright © 2021 Linda Wimes

Published by Linda Wimes
P.O. Box 10025
Dothan, AL 36304

ISBN: 978-1-7366255-1-4

Cover and Interior Design by Ebony Horton
Cover Photos by Sherline Hudson and Dee Spivey (Shine Your Light Photography)
Printed in the United States of America

DEDICATION

This book is dedicated to all who face various doors in life and need hope and encouragement. It's to those of you who don't know what to do when you encounter these doors. You don't know whether to open or close them, or just stay in your present state of being depressed, afraid, disappointed, abandoned, abused, neglected, broken, or torn.

These doors are real and may be hard to handle, but you don't have to face them alone.

This book is also dedicated to our "children" who I have come to love as mine with my involvement with HIS Prison Ministries. You've had to face many doors that were thrust upon you. You did not ask for the fate that life dealt you. You are not forgotten, and you are not alone. You are so special to God and to us. We love you.

TABLE OF CONTENTS

Foreword by Ivorye Perry
Introduction

Sources
Resources and Scriptures
Acknowledgments
About the Author

FOREWORD

When asked to write the foreword for this book, my initial reaction was an overwhelming sense of anxiety. I didn't want to think about doors in life – especially the doors that had closed. It was too hard. As my mind started to spin, Mrs. Wimes, who I affectionately call "Ms. Linda", immediately began to speak life into me. She said, "God told me to tell you that you are qualified." To hear those words and to know the type of unwavering faith that Ms. Linda has, there wasn't a doubt in my mind that she, indeed, had heard directly from Him. I took "you are qualified" to mean, "You can handle it. You won't fall apart." God's grace carries us through door after door. It's a blessing to be able to glorify God! Don't be hesitant; have faith in Him.

Doors represent many things, as you will learn in Ms. Linda's book. Personally, I have had my share of doors: grief, loss, and hopelessness. How do we handle these doors knowing that our choices not only affect us but the lives of others? I believe this book will not only breathe hope into the doors we face, but will also serve as a reminder that even in the depths of hopelessness, God will never leave you. The people in this book have all wrestled with doors of fear, sadness, and disappointment. They've also found God right there with them. May we all open up our hearts and learn from the people in this book. May we each be moved by how they trusted and believed in God's promises, despite the door.

When you read this book, expect to feel challenged, convicted, and to find yourself wondering how Ms. Linda knows you and all your business! This book helps us to see how we can face the doors in our own lives, confidently knowing that God is there with us. As unworthy as we may feel and as imperfect as we are, God will still use our doors for our good and His glory. We can place our hope and faith in the Lord!

- Ivorye Perry

INTRODUCTION

Doors are everywhere. Your house, my house, and every house has at least one. These doors either allow movement forward or prevent movement. They are a symbol of duality, as a door is either closed or open, locked or unlocked. Any time we encounter a door, we find that we have to make a choice.

In addition to physical doors, there are mental doors that we must choose how we will enter or leave. Who faces these doors? In one way or another, all of us: the bruised and broken-hearted, those suffering in silence, those suffering from loneliness, the parents whose child is addicted to drugs, the abused, the neglected or abandoned, the loveless, the let-down, the broken families, the rejected, those suffering illness, those suffering loss, the unemployed, and the list goes on.

What if I told you that the door you are facing right now is bound to set you on a path to fulfillment of God's purpose in your life and genuine joy? I know it sounds crazy. But whether you believe me or not, there are stories of doors all throughout the next several pages that are aimed to show you this truth.

The doors in this book represent many areas of our lives from the view of similar doors in scripture and from the testimonies of people who were willing to share their stories. There are doors of loss, uncertainties, disappointments, abuse, hurt, pain, depression, loneliness, unforgiveness, compromise, and addiction. These are the doors such as Phyllis encountered starting from the age of 3 of being unwanted, raped, and abused. Seeing no way out, she had thoughts of ending her life. There is also the kind of door that Robert walked through that closed behind him with a heartbreaking consequence, but taught him a valuable lesson that would impact the rest of his life.

I, too, have had my share of doors and have made some major life-or-death choices as a result of them. I share some of them in this book. The full story of one of my major doors is found in our first book, *You Have To Be Willing To Die: Don't Be*

Moved By What You Hear, when I refused cancer treatments for a prognosis years ago that could have ended in death. I faced what could have been a similar door while writing this book.

Your decision to read this book lets me know that you are at a point where you have doors and choices to make, too, and that you're not one to give up easily. In the same way that doors opened an opportunity for others to be blessed by our stories, I believe that this book will unveil hope in your life and cause you to see that God is willing to be with you as you face the doors you encounter. And guess what else? He will work them for your good.

Even though we walk through the valley of the shadow of death, we don't have to fear evil because He is with us (Psalm 23). Listen, the valley is a shadow of death. A shadow is not real. It's just blocking the light. The Light of the World overshadows darkness every time.

We cannot deny that sometimes having hope can be hard to do when you're going through a difficult door. In this book, you'll be encouraged to stop looking at your current circumstances and look to the One who can and is willing to walk you through them. I am talking about the One, the Light of the World, who knows, even before we do, that we are weak and hurting. Allow me to introduce you to Him. His name is Jesus. He stands with open arms to embrace – with you – whatever you are facing. He is our hope. He has you.

In this book, you will observe that just as Abraham and others in the Bible and in this book, you, too, can have hope in the Lord and not be disappointed (Isaiah 49:23). You see, God is faithful (Hebrews 10:23), He doesn't lie (Numbers 23:19), He doesn't forget, and you can be confident in knowing He does just what He says. Keep hoping and don't be discouraged or give in because your future is much brighter than it may appear right now.

As you travel through this book, you will find lots of scriptures. They are life-giving. But don't just take my word. Go examine the scriptures for yourself to see if what is said is true.

You will also find sections called a "Pause Break." Take the time and ponder what has been said. Expect to be reminded time and time again that:

- You are not alone.
- He will face the doors with you.
- He will use your doors for your good and His glory.

Allow God to be in complete control. He, alone, opens doors no one can shut and shuts doors no one can open. He will open doors as He sees fit and close doors that He doesn't want you going through. And He will use them for your good and His glory.

I encourage you to open the door of your heart and trust Him. You don't have to face your doors alone. He wants to come in and face the doors with you:

Here I am! I stand at the door and knock. If anyone hears my voice and opens the door, I will come in and eat with that person, and they with me.
-Revelation 3:20

JOSEPH'S DOORS

Have you heard of Joseph? I'm talking about the one in the Bible. My 6-year old's story about Joseph would sound like this:

"He's that boy with a bunch of brothers. They didn't like him. One day, they threw him in a hole in the ground. Then somebody else came and got him out. Then he was in jail. Then…then, he went somewhere else and…and, he was sitting on the top. He wasn't in the hole no more."

Is this the Joseph you heard of? Well, here's my grown-up version of Joseph's story: Joseph was born in the Mesopotamian town of Haran. His father is Jacob (also known as Israel) and his mother is Rachael. His father had 13 children – 12 sons and one daughter – by four different women. Joseph was the 11th son. At the age of 6, he left Haran along with his family and journeyed to the land of Canaan.[1]

Joseph's father loved him more than all his sons because he was born to him in his old age. He even made Joseph a special robe. These factors caused Joseph's brothers to be jealous of him: "They hated him and could not speak a kind word to him" (Genesis 37:4). They all lived together as one big family. Notice I said one "big" family, not one big, happy family.

One day, Joseph had two dreams and shared them with his brothers. The dreams implied that he would one day be superior and rule over them (Genesis 37:5-10). I don't know if telling them was the wisest thing to do. I can't think of any sibling who would want the other sibling to say, "I am going to rule over you". The scripture says, "…They hated him all the more because of his dream and what he said" (verse 5). Their hate was intense to the point of wanting to harm him.

Joseph appears to be naïve about his brothers' feelings toward him. Was he off in his own world, walking around as his father's favorite son and wearing his special robe? How could he not sense the disconnect? Would you think something is wrong if a sibling did not speak a kind word to you?

These brothers did not hide their feelings and were waiting for the right moment to deal with Joseph on their own terms. That opportunity came when Joseph's father sent him to check on his brothers and bring word back to him.

JOSEPH'S BROTHERS

Joseph traveled and found his brothers near Dothan (not Dothan, Alabama). His brothers saw him from a distance. They took matters into their own hands and plotted to kill Joseph.

"Here comes that dreamer!" they said to each other. "Come now, let's kill him and throw him into one of these cisterns and say that a ferocious animal devoured him. Then we'll see what comes of his dreams."
-Genesis 37:19-20

Reuben, the oldest brother, convinced them to throw Joseph in the pit alive. He intended to come back later and save him. When Joseph arrived, his brothers stripped off his robe and threw him into the empty pit. Joseph is probably going crazy trying to figure out what they're going to do to him. Can you imagine him pleading for his life, "No, no, don't do this? Brothers, don't do this to me"? It was 10 of them against a helpless young, 17-year-old Joseph. A good whipping wouldn't be as final as a killing. How could they live with themselves? Were they afraid Joseph's dream might really happen and they would bow before him? Oh, how deep the brothers hated Joseph.

Joseph's brothers sat down to eat their meal after throwing him into the pit. Then, they noticed a caravan of Ishmaelites coming from Gilead.

The Ishmaelites were like traveling salesmen. They had items that they would buy, sell, or trade with people as they traveled from one place to another. So, Joseph's brother Judah suggested selling Joseph to the Ishmaelites instead of killing him, and the rest of the brothers (except Reuben) agreed. Does this sound like human trafficking to you?

They lifted Joseph out of the pit. He is probably relieved to be out and ready to go home, but his freedom is short-lived because his brothers (except Reuben) have other plans. They sold him to the Ishmaelites for 20 shekels of silver. According to the foreign exchange rate for today, it would equal $6.17. From there, Joseph was taken to Egypt and purchased (no price given) by one of Pharaoh's officials. How difficult it must have been for Joseph to experience a brief freedom from the pit just to face *another* door! Can you imagine how he was feeling while being carried away?

In one moment, Joseph's life was forever changed by someone else's actions. He went from the favor of his father to being sold like a piece of meat in the market. His heart must have raced as his mind wondered why. His future and life were uncertain. Only the Lord knew what fate awaited him.

JOSEPH'S MASTER

Joseph remained faithful to the Lord in spite of being removed from his home, and the Lord was with him. Even while Joseph was a slave, he prospered. Genesis 39:2-6 says:

... When his master saw that the LORD was with him and that the LORD gave him success in everything he did, Joseph found favor in his eyes and became his attendant. Potiphar put him in charge of his household, and he entrusted to his care everything he owned. From the time he put him in charge of his household and of all that he owned, the LORD blessed the household of the Egyptian because of Joseph. The blessing of the LORD was on everything Potiphar had, both in the house and in the field. So Potiphar left everything he had in Joseph's care; with Joseph in charge, he did not

concern himself with anything except the food he ate.

While God was with and watching over Joseph, someone else was watching this well-built and handsome young man, too: Potiphar's wife. She wanted to sleep with Joseph, but he refused. He wanted to honor his master and God (Genesis 39:7-12). It didn't seem to matter to her. Day after day, she continued to hound Joseph like a dog in heat. This sounds like a good case of sexual harassment to me. Joseph still refused. But this woman wouldn't give up. She wanted what she wanted.

Let's pause for a second for some good advice. When you find yourself in a position or at a door to do right or wrong, do right. Don't become entangled with wrong. Leave whatever you have to behind and get out.

Now back to Potiphar's wife. She was upset and fit to be tied when Joseph did not consent to her request. She wanted him to pay and came up with her story (lies). She told the household servants:

"...this Hebrew has been brought to us to make sport of us! He came in here to sleep with me, but I screamed. When he heard me scream for help, he left his cloak beside me and ran out of the house."
-Genesis 39:14-15

She waited for Potiphar to return and repeated the same story to him. Potiphar was angry. He didn't ask Joseph for his side of the story. But then, who would believe a slave, anyway? There was no deliberation. Potiphar was Joseph's judge. He found him guilty as charged and sent him to prison where the king's prisoners were confined instead of having Joseph executed for the crime for which he was being accused. Maybe Potiphar had some doubts about his wife's story. He was still obligated to act on them.

Now, Joseph faces another door. He is in prison based on a one-sided story fabricated by a lying woman who didn't get what she wanted. Joseph may not have known if he would ever be released. His status changes again. But God is about to use this door for good.

FROM SLAVERY, BIG DREAMS

Joseph's journey thus far has been one crazy trip. I'm not sure which is worse: being a slave or prisoner. Yet, what seems like misery to the human eye was not all that was at work. Remember, God was still with Joseph:

...But while Joseph was there in the prison, the LORD was with him; he showed him kindness and granted him favor in the eyes of the prison warden. So the warden put Joseph in charge of all those held in the prison, and he was made responsible for all that was done there. The warden paid no attention to anything under Joseph's care, because the LORD was with Joseph and gave him success in whatever he did.
-Genesis 39:20-23

No matter Joseph's circumstance, the Lord gave Joseph success in whatever he did. Why? Because Joseph remained faithful to God. While in prison, Joseph was assigned Pharaoh's cupbearer and baker (Genesis 40). One day, Joseph saw that they had long faces and asked why. They told him they had dreamed dreams but had no one to interpret them. Joseph says, "Do not interpretations belong to God? Tell me your dreams."

Let's pause here for a moment. Would you be interested in dreams if you were in Joseph's situation? If I was Joseph, I wouldn't want to hear anything about dreams at all. It was his dream that caused his brothers to hate him more. Now, these two people want to know the interpretations of their dream? I think I would have told them, "I'll pray for you." But Joseph's actions show he didn't think about himself, his dreams, or his status as a slave in prison. As a result, God gave Joseph the interpretation.

Joseph told the cupbearer that Pharaoh would reinstate him to his position within three days. Joseph also told the cupbearer his own story of being forcibly carried from the land of the Hebrews and that he had done nothing deserving of being put in a dungeon. He asked the cupbearer to remember him and mention him to Pharaoh to get him out of prison.

While the interpretation of the cupbearer's dream was a positive one, there was something different in store for the chief baker. Joseph told the chief baker that within three days Pharaoh would lift the baker's head and hang his body on a pole. Then, the birds would eat away his flesh. Both dreams happened in real life as Joseph interpreted, but the cupbearer did not remember Joseph; he forgot him. Days and months passed, and Joseph remained in prison...for another two years.

Even though the cupbearer forgot about Joseph, God didn't. There's about to be another door for Joseph.

Later, Pharaoh ends up having some troubling dreams (Genesis 41). No one could interpret them for him. The cupbearer's memory returns and he remembers Joseph. He tells the Pharaoh about the prison encounter, and as a result, Pharoah sends for Joseph. Pharaoh tells Joseph his dream and that he heard that he could interpret it. Joseph told Pharaoh that he couldn't interpret dreams but God would give him the answer he desires. Pharaoh tells Joseph the dream and God gives the interpretation. Joseph advises Pharoah to "look for a discerning and wise man and put him in charge of the land of Egypt and ... appoint commissioners over the land to take a fifth of the harvest of Egypt during the seven years of abundance" (verses 33-34). Pharaoh liked Joseph's suggestion. God was about to show Joseph some more favor.

FROM DREAMS TO THE PALACE

It may have felt like a long time coming, but Pharaoh discerned something different about Joseph. He said to Joseph:

"Since God has made all this known to you, there is no one so discerning and wise as you. You shall be in charge of my palace, and all my people are to submit to your orders. Only with respect to the

throne will I be greater than you." So Pharaoh said to Joseph, "I hereby put you in charge of the whole land of Egypt." Then Pharaoh took his signet ring from his finger and put it on Joseph's finger. He dressed him in robes of fine linen and put a gold chain around his neck. He had him ride in a chariot as his second-in-command, and people shouted before him, "Make way!" Thus he put him in charge of the whole land of Egypt.
-Genesis 41:39-43

Wow. Look at Joseph's new position: second-in-command. Wait a minute. Is this happening again? A slave with no rights becomes the one who has favor in his master's eyes. He was a slave who remained faithful to God and refused to have sex with his master's wife, who in turn lied on him. He was a slave on his way to prison for a crime he didn't commit. And now, the favored son, slave, and innocent prisoner, is second-in-command in charge of the whole land of Egypt. And one more thing: he only answers to Pharaoh. No middleman this time!

As the dream predicted in Genesis 41, the famine spread over the whole country and Joseph opened all the storehouses. People came from everywhere to Egypt. Guess who is among them?

JOSEPH'S BROTHERS, AGAIN

In full circle, we see Joseph's brothers again. The famine led them to Egypt to buy food. Who's in charge, and who do they get to bow low before? They had no idea it was their younger brother, Joseph. They had no idea it was the one their father favored and they hated. Joseph, the one they wanted to kill but sold into slavery, and the one they thought they would never encounter again, would be the one to save them. Never would they have imagined the fulfillment of Joseph's dream coming to pass. Now, they are about to see what became of the dreams of the dreamer.

Although they didn't recognize Joseph, he recognized them. He also remembered his dream about them. Still, he did not make himself known to them initially. He questioned and put them to the test. Their consciences bothered them as he questioned them:

They said to one another, "Surely we are being punished because of our brother. We saw how distressed he was when he pleaded with us for his life, but we would not listen; that's why this distress has come on us." Reuben replied, "Didn't I tell you not to sin against the boy? But you wouldn't listen! Now we must give an accounting for his blood."
-Genesis 42:21-22

The brothers left Joseph's presence feeling bewildered. One of them opened his sack to feed his donkey and discovered that his silver had been returned. When he told his brothers, their hearts sank, and they turned to each other trembling and said, "What is this that God has done to us?" (Genesis 42:28). Is it ironic to you that they question what God has done to them? Yet, it doesn't appear they had any thought of God when they sold Joseph into slavery.

The brothers arrived home and told their father everything about their trip to Egypt. The famine was still severe and they ran out of food. Their father told them to go back to Egypt to buy some more food. This time they had to bring Benjamin, Joseph's brother, with them. They came before Joseph and after some interaction, Joseph made himself known to his brothers.

Joseph said to his brothers, "I am Joseph! Is my father still living?" But his brothers were not able to answer him, because they were terrified at his presence. Then Joseph said to his brothers, "Come close to me." When they had done so, he said, "I am your brother Joseph, the one you sold into Egypt! And now, do not be distressed and do not be angry with yourselves for selling me here, because it was to save lives that God sent me ahead of you. For two years now there has been famine in the land, and for the next five years there will be no plowing and reaping. But God sent me ahead of you to preserve for you a remnant on earth and to save your lives by

a great deliverance. "So then, it was not you who sent me here, but God. He made me father to Pharaoh, lord of his entire household and ruler of all Egypt. ..."
-Genesis 45:3-11

The word reached Pharaoh. He said to Joseph:

"...Tell your brothers, 'Do this: Load your animals and return to the land of Canaan, and bring your father and your families back to me. I will give you the best of the land of Egypt and you can enjoy the fat of the land.'
-Genesis 45:17-18

Do you see how God's favor on Joseph benefitted his father and family?

Pharaoh said to Joseph, "Your father and your brothers have come to you, and the land of Egypt is before you; settle your father and your brothers in the best part of the land. Let them live in Goshen...."
-Genesis 47:5-6

Joseph made sure they were well taken care of.

A door that was intended for harm allowed Joseph to be in the right place and position at the right time when his family needed him most. The position revealed in his dream as a boy was true, and both his father and brothers were able to witness and benefit from it.

Of course, Joseph had every reason to reject his brothers. It is clear in scripture that the brothers were concerned about the roles being reversed. No longer was it 10-to-one. Joseph was now The One. Maybe his brothers saw the handwriting on the wall for their lives. It is for sure it was on their minds because they spoke to their father (so they said) about it before he died. They even said to Joseph, "We are your slaves" (Genesis 50:16-18).

Hold up. Wait a minute. It appears that the script is flipped from the brothers saying, "Do you intend to reign over us? Will you actually rule us?" to them bowing low to him and saying, "We are your slaves". Look at Joseph's response:

"...Don't be afraid. Am I in the place of God? You intended to harm me, but God intended it for good to accomplish what is now being done, the saving of many lives. So then, don't be afraid. I will provide for you and your children." And he reassured them and spoke kindly to them.
-Genesis 50:19-21

Pause Break – Pause Break!

Joseph's brothers meant to harm him. They knew what it meant to sell him into slavery. Even as I write, I am feeling some kind of way towards these brothers. I'm thinking about the way they treated Joseph, and now they are needing his help. However, this horrible act would be the door by which Joseph's dream would be fulfilled. Have you or someone you know been in a situation where someone was wronged and the perpetrator later needed help? How was it handled?

THE MAN, HIS GOD, AND THE PROMISE

Joseph's story is a reminder of the movies with the villains and good guys. The good guys seem to endure lots of tragedy but in the end, they win. Joseph is our good guy. Even when it seemed like he was losing, he won every time. The Lord was always with him, regardless of the doors he faced. Let's look again at every time God was with Him:

In Potiphar's House
The LORD was with Joseph so that he prospered, and he lived in the house of his Egyptian master.
-Genesis 39:2

In Prison
The LORD was with him; he showed him kindness and granted him favor in the eyes of the prison warden.
-Genesis 39:21

The warden paid no attention to anything under Joseph's care, because the LORD was with Joseph and gave him success in whatever he did.
-Genesis 39:23

In the Palace (Pharaoh)
You shall be in charge of my palace, and all my people are to submit to your orders. ....
-Genesis 41:40

So Pharaoh said to Joseph, "I hereby put you in charge of the whole land of Egypt."
-Genesis 41:41

There is more to Joseph's story in Genesis 37-50, but you can see from the pieces that I have shared that Joseph's story is *our* story. The doors he faced are similar to the same doors we encounter. As we travel through the chapters in this book with the stories from scripture and from people today, we will use Joseph's story as an example of how we can handle the doors we face – the good, bad, and ugly doors.

Just as Joseph remained faithful to God and God was with him, God is no respecter of persons and is willing to be with you. He will help you face the doors meant for bad, for your good, and for His glory.

DOORS OF OUR HEART

When we hear the word, "heart", we immediately think of the vessel behind our chest. And rightfully so because that's the one we learned about in school. I even thought that was where love came from. Now that I'm older, I understand that we have two hearts. You have the physical heart, and the other one is our spiritual heart. In this chapter, we will discuss both, their importance, and the correlation between them.

First, let me present my credentials to do so. I am not a physical heart specialist. We have well-educated doctors who specialize in that field. Neither am I a spiritual heart specialist. We have an all-knowing God who specializes in this field. There aren't any letters behind my name. I am an ordinary woman who loves God, who is willing to seek after him and to share with others about His love for each of us. That's it. I've researched the information I share in this chapter and felt like I was back in school. And you may, too. I'm learning things I didn't know or had forgotten. Now that that's settled, let's learn together how to check out our hearts.

Man is a triune being created in the image of God, composed of spirit, soul, and body (1 Thessalonians 5:23). The body contains the soul, but a body is dead without the spirit (James 2:26). A soul gets its life in a body with the help of the spirit. That makes the heart essential to all three – spirit, soul, and body.

The physical heart is an organ that supplies blood to the body. The spiritual heart nourishes a soul through which God interacts with man. This sounds a little confusing, doesn't it? It did to me. I had to search other scriptures to gain a better understanding. They're in the back of this book.

However, the bottom line is this: both the physical and spiritual hearts are important.

THE PHYSICAL HEART

Science was not my favorite subject in school and researching the human heart reminds me why. However, I am very appreciative of those who have an interest in the heart and can educate us on how to keep it healthy and pumping. This research of the heart has given me a better understanding of why my doctor checks the status of my heart at every visit. He can listen to it, check my heart rate, and check my blood pressure. I welcome it so we can make sure each pulse is matching up with a heartbeat that pumps blood through my arteries. If you don't appreciate your heart or your doctor checking it, let me recommend you do a little research, too.

The heart is one of the most important organs in our body. It's about the size of your fist. It pumps blood through your body to provide it with the oxygen and nutrients it needs to survive. If the heart is not able to supply blood to the organs and tissues, they'll die. And if they die, we know what happens next. Leviticus 17:11 reminds us that the life of a creature is in the blood. Therefore, your physical heart is the difference between keeping or stopping the flow of your life. That's how important it is.

Now, the doctor's examination of our physical heart is strictly from the physical aspect. He does not consider the spiritual heart. That's God's business. As a matter of fact, God knows every human heart (1 Kings 8:39) and tests them, too (Proverbs 17:3).

THE SPIRITUAL HEART

The spiritual heart is part of man's spiritual makeup. It is the place where emotions and desires begin; it is that which drives the will of man towards action. The spiritual heart is the seat of our will, intellect, and feelings.

We must guard our spiritual heart. Jeremiah 17:9-10 says:

The heart is deceitful above all things and beyond cure. Who can understand it? "I the LORD search the heart and examine the mind, to reward each person according to their conduct, according to what their deeds deserve."

Jesus said, "For it is from within, out of a person's heart, that evil thoughts come — sexual immorality, theft, murder, adultery, greed, malice, deceit, lewdness, envy, slander, arrogance and folly" (Mark 7:21-22). In Luke 6:45, Jesus says, "A good man brings good things out of the good stored up in his heart, and an evil man brings evil things out of the evil stored up in his heart. For the mouth speaks what the heart is full of." This sounds like what I've heard my elders say: "Honey, what's in ya', going to come out ya'." In other words, whatever is within your spiritual heart will come out of you in your words and actions.

Proverbs 23:7 and Proverbs 27:19 help us to understand that our thoughts dictate who we become because our minds reflect who we are. The Lord examines our heart. He knows the depths of them and sees into the inner motivations of the heart.

Another way of saying it is, "People look at the outward appearance, but the Lord looks at the heart" (1 Samuel 16:7).

The heart is the center not only of spiritual activity but of all the operations of human life. King Solomon says our heart is the "wellspring of life" (Proverbs 4:23). A wellspring is the head or source of a spring, stream, or river. Just as the wellspring, your heart is the source of everything else – your heart overflows into thoughts, words, and actions.

Your heart is the core of your being. It is that part of you that connects with God and other people. It must be guarded.

GUARD YOUR HEART

Both our physical and spiritual heart are designed in such a way that they can grow any type of seed, no matter if the seed is good or bad. A seed carries within itself new life. However, it has to be buried before it can bring it forth.

In the same way, both the physical and spiritual heart are constantly under attack. Sometimes these attacks are subtle. That is why we must be on watch. We must guard what is being planted in our hearts. We must protect it in the same way we protect ourselves against physical sicknesses of the world. Just as the precautions surrounding coronavirus, we've been warned regarding sickness to:

- Avoid people who are sick.
- Wash your hands well and often.
- Clean surfaces and objects that people touch a lot (like doorknobs and countertops).
- Try not to touch your eyes, nose, and mouth.

What is interesting about these warnings is that there is some correlation to protecting our spiritual heart. Think about it. Do you want to be around those who are spiritually sick, who are not constantly being washed and renewed by the Word of God, and are therefore "contaminated"? They could cause you to be sick with their worries, hesitations, and misery. I have no desire to be sick. Do you? Then, we should do our best to avoid as much contact as possible.

Do you see yet why our spiritual hearts must be guarded? We have seen in the lives of others – and possibly our own – the results of not guarding our hearts. Observe the negative treatment of some people towards others who do not resemble them, share their beliefs, or of the same political party, for example. They're contaminated, and we will be, too, if we do not avoid them. First Corinthians 15:33 says, "Do not be misled: Bad company corrupts good character." So, when it comes to partnering with bad company, remember this statement from Joe in Tyler Perry's movie, *Madea's Family Reunion* (2006): "Don't Do It". Your heart and your life are at stake, and others may be affected or infected. That's something to think about, isn't it?

Joseph's heart could have been bitter. After all, look at the way he had been treated. He dealt with his misfortunes differently. His story serves as a reminder of the importance of guarding the doors of our hearts.

Pause Break – Pause Break!

Look at the guards placed during COVID-19. They were not there for harm, but for our safety. How much more important is it that we guard our heart since the issues of life flow from it? What did you notice about Joseph's heart as he was confronted with the different doors?

The emotional state of the heart affects the rest of a person: "A happy heart makes the face cheerful, but heartache crushes the spirit (Proverb 15:13); "A cheerful heart is good medicine, but a crushed spirit dries up the bones" (Proverb 17:22).

A study from John Hopkins, The Power of Positive Thinking, stated the following:[2]

"People with a family history of heart disease who also had a positive outlook were one-third less likely to have a heart attack or other cardiovascular event within five to 25 years than those with a more negative outlook. The mechanism for the connection between health and positivity remains murky, but researchers suspect that people who are more positive may be better protected against the inflammatory damage of stress. Another possibility is that hope and positivity help people make better health and life decisions and focus more on long-term goals. Studies also find that negative emotions can weaken immune response.

What is clear, however, is that there is definitely a strong link between 'positivity' and health. Additional studies have found that a positive attitude improves outcomes and life satisfaction across a spectrum of conditions – including traumatic brain injury, stroke and brain tumors."

Do you want to maintain a healthy heart? Then, you have to be alert to what enters and dwells there. What we say and do and who we become is the result of the state of our hearts.

We are in a fight for our very lives. The attacks are going to come. We have to be on guard and prepare for them. Ephesians 6:10-18 calls it a fight to the finish and tells us how to stay in the battle. The Message version states it this way:

And that about wraps it up. God is strong, and he wants you strong. So take everything the Master has set out for you, well-made weapons of the best materials. And put them to use so you will be able to stand up to everything the Devil throws your way. This is no weekend war that we'll walk away from and forget about in a couple of hours. This is for keeps, a life-or-death fight to the finish against the Devil and all his angels. Be prepared. You're up against far more than you can handle on your own. Take all the help you can get, every weapon God has issued, so that when it's all over but the shouting you'll still be on your feet. Truth, righteousness, peace, faith, and salvation are more than words. Learn how to apply them. You'll need them throughout your life. God's Word is an indispensable weapon. In the same way, prayer is essential in this ongoing warfare. Pray hard and long. Pray for your brothers and sisters. Keep your eyes open. Keep each other's spirits up so that no one falls behind or drops out.

Again, the attacks are coming. The secret is out. And it makes no difference whether we're ready or not. The enemy is on his job to steal, kill, and destroy (John 10:10). He's seeking whomever he can devour. It can be a struggle to guard our heart, but it is one of those things we must do, like eating food to nourish our bodies. As a good soldier in battle, we must prepare and be on guard for the attack.

THE HEART ATTACK

Do you remember Fred from the television show *Sanford and Son*? Fred would place his hand over his chest and say, "You hear that Elizabeth? I'm comin' to join ya' honey!" As we know, he was just faking to get his way. A heart attack is real and doesn't exactly happen like Fred's.

According to the Centers for Disease Control and Prevention, heart disease is the leading cause of death in the United States, causing about one in four deaths. Every 40 seconds, someone in the United States has a heart attack. Several health conditions – your lifestyle, your age and family history – can increase your risk for heart disease and heart attack. These are called risk factors.

About half of all Americans have at least one of the three key risk factors for heart disease: high blood pressure, high blood cholesterol, and smoking. A heart attack happens when a part of the heart muscle doesn't get enough blood. In the United States, coronary artery disease (CAD) is the main cause of heart attack. The major symptoms of a heart attack are chest pain or discomfort; feeling weak, light-headed, or faint; pain or discomfort in the jaw, neck, or back; pain or discomfort in one or both arms or shoulders; and shortness of breath. Other symptoms could include unusual or unexplained tiredness and nausea, vomiting, or breaking out in a cold sweat.[3] Have you ever had any of these symptoms or noticed them in someone else? Even if you're not sure it's a heart attack, or even if the symptoms feel subtle, immediately call 911. I had some of these symptoms and went to my doctor. It wasn't a heart attack. I'm thankful it was just menopause, but it was still worth checking out.

It would be to our benefit to learn to recognize the symptoms of a physical and spiritual heart attack. Every heart attack can be different. The onset of a physical heart attack can be more subtle. It could start slowly with mild pain or discomfort. It shows up like a thief in the night. We never know when a thief is coming, right?

Symptoms of a spiritual heart attack show up as a difference in your walk with the Lord. Your heart becomes easily swayed by the influence of the world. You begin to have a lack of love for God and lack of desire for a continual relationship with Him. The things of God, such as fellowshipping with other believers, prayer, and the Word of God, are no longer important to you. You find yourself compromising lies for the Truth.

The physical symptom of restlessness is another indicator of a possible heart attack. You are uncomfortable when you lie down, sit or stand; you are unable to find any physical comfort or rest. Spiritually, the same is true in your walk of faith. The inability to be still before the Lord is an indicator that you are restless. You become impatient and no longer wait on the Lord for guidance. You start to lean on your own understanding and begin to walk according to your flesh, which is opposed to God (Romans 8:7).

Plaque build-up in the coronary arteries is another symptom identified as bad cholesterol. It causes blockage of the blood flow to the heart. Likewise, continual and unrepentant sin robs you of fellowship with God; it separates you from Him. Isaiah 59:2 says, "But your iniquities have separated you from your God; your sins have hidden His face from you, so that he will not hear." The children of Israel were constantly forgetting God. Turning their backs on Him became their norm. He warned them time after time. They would repent and go right back to their ways. However, we can't be too hard on them because we find ourselves being no different at times.

Sin in the spiritual heart is similar to the plaque build-up that causes blockage of the blood flow to the physical heart. Ezekiel 18:20 reminds us that the soul who sins shall die. It is so important to learn to identify the symptoms of spiritual heart disease, but also to understand the risks associated with each symptom. If not addressed, your risk of developing a spiritual, life-threatening heart condition will develop. This includes a broken heart.

THE BROKEN HEART

Everyone, at some point in our life, has experienced a broken heart to some degree. I say this because no one is perfect (except God). We all have not given or received love perfectly. Think for a moment when your heart was broken. Was it not because someone who verbalized love or care for you did not act like you thought he or she should have? I feel certain that Joseph's heart was broken by his brothers' actions. Wouldn't yours be? A heart that is broken carries a pain that is both physical and spiritual.

A broken heart is a serious matter. It's not as simple and beautiful as Al Green sings in the song, "How Can You Mend A Broken Heart?" that was written by Barry and Robin Gibb. Not all people can see past the rain from falling down, the sun from shining, or a loser ever winning. Other conditions, such as fear, anger, hopelessness, hardness, or numbness may occur in the heart when brokenness is left ignored.

According to the American Heart Association, broken heart syndrome – or takotsubo cardiomyopathy – is a reaction your heart has to a surge of stress hormones caused by an emotionally stressful event. That event could be due to the death of a person or a relationship: the death of a loved one or the pain of a divorce, breakup or physical separation, betrayal, or romantic rejection. Broken heart syndrome could even happen after a good shock, like winning the lottery. Broken heart syndrome causes the heart to stop operating normally, resulting in heart failure. During these situations, the body releases an increase of hormones, which temporarily paralyze your heart and limit its standard functionality. Most people who experience it make a full recovery within weeks, and they're at low risk of it happening again (although in rare cases it can be fatal).

A real-life broken heart can actually lead to cardiac consequences, too. There are established ties among depression, mental health, and heart disease. Broken heart syndrome symptoms can even mimic a heart attack. The most common signs and symptoms of broken heart syndrome are angina (chest pain) and shortness of breath. You can experience these things even if you have no history of heart disease.[4] As another disclaimer, any long-lasting or persistent chest pain could be a sign of a heart attack, so it's important to take it seriously and seek medical attention if you experience chest pain. Do not ignore these physical symptoms.

What can be done, then, about a broken heart? How can it be mended? How can it be healed? For sure, the answer is not a song or time. A song can only last but so long and time surely doesn't heal it. There's only one source who can comfort and heal a broken heart. He is the Great Physician. He wants to heal the doors of your heart.

He heals the brokenhearted and binds up their wounds.
-Psalm 147:3

You're not alone in any heartbreak you have experienced. You don't have to suffer in silence. If you have not already, it's time to face the pain you've kept inside. Grieve through what you did not allow yourself to grieve. Just as you go to the dentist for treatment of an abscessed tooth, you can come to the Great Physician for any condition and be healed. Aren't you tired of the pain eating away at you? Then, come on.

The LORD is close to the brokenhearted and saves those who are crushed in spirit.
-Psalm 34:18

My flesh and my heart may fail, but God is the strength of my heart and my portion forever.
-Psalm 73:26

It's time to have your broken heart healed. Your appointment has been scheduled. All you have to do is show up. You can have as many appointments as needed, free of charge. Just show up!

In addition to reading the scriptures, there are other resources that can offer support. We can lean on others to get through this life. The Bible tells us to bear one another's burdens (Galatians 6:2) and encourage one another and build each other up (1 Thessalonians 5:11). If you need further help, talk to a counselor or a trusted friend. There are additional resources in the back of this book that you can browse through, too, for guidance.

HEART CHECK-UP

We're told that we need a regular health check-up. We definitely do need a regular heart check-up. Everything physical and spiritual flows from the heart. We need to ensure that there is no blockage that restricts a positive flow.

When is the last time you've checked your heart? What instrument or standard did you use? Did you check your pulse and find it matching up with a heartbeat? Here comes the big question: did you find your heart to be healthy (physically) and pure (spiritually)?

In the Bible, David prayed that God would create in him a pure heart (Psalm 51:10). Pure is not mixed or adulterated with any other substance or material. It is free of any contamination. David wanted his heart genuine, real, clean, germ-free, uncorrupted, authentic, and virtuous. This should become one of our prayers, too. Let's see what was going on that caused David to recognize that his heart needed to be pure. Second Samuel 11 tells us that King David saw Bathsheba, a married woman, and lusted after her. He summoned her to fulfill his desires. Sometime later, she notified him that she was pregnant with his child. David first tried a cover-up scheme.

When that did not work, he arranged for the murder of Bathsheba's husband. David then married her. This displeased the Lord.

God sent Nathan, the prophet, to confront David (2 Samuel 12). Nathan used a parable that David could relate to. He told of a rich man who took advantage of a poor man by stealing his only lamb, a pet, which he killed to feed to his guests. David was overcome with anger and said, "As surely as the Lord lives, the man who did this must die! He must pay for that lamb four times over, because he did such a thing and had no pity" (2 Samuel 12:5–6).

Nathan responded to David, "You are the man!" (2 Samuel 12:7).

You see, when David initially tried to hide his sin, it signaled a blockage of the blood flow to his heart. After he was confronted, David recognized the blockage, faced the door, and admitted to Nathan, "I have sinned against the Lord" (2 Samuel 12:13). David did not want his heart to stop flowing. Sin will stop the flow. David knew he needed a clean heart.

Do you see how much God loved David and wouldn't let this matter go unchecked? Doesn't this sound like a check-up? He loves us just as much. Our God understands the importance of keeping the wellspring of life – our heart – flowing.

God knew David's heart and testified about him: "'I have found David son of Jesse, a man after my own heart; he will do everything I want him to do'" (Acts 13:22). David repented and received forgiveness. Forgiveness is freedom and it allows our heart to freely flow.

The Bible says, "...People look at the outward appearance, but the LORD looks at the heart" (1 Samuel 16:7). When God looks at a man, He doesn't look at the clothes he wears, the color of his skin, or his social status. The Lord weighs our heart (Proverbs 21:2). He sees and knows our thoughts, motives, and intents.

A LITTLE OBSERVATION

Travel with me through 2 Samuel 13 and 14 and let's observe some more hearts. It begins with Amnon, the oldest son of David, falling in love with Tamar, his half-sister (same father, different mother). He was so obsessed with her that he made himself sick. He knew Tamar was a virgin and he couldn't see how he could get his hands on her. I am convinced that Amnon also knew it was wrong and not lawful. The oldest of David's sons, you would think Amnon knew or heard of God's specific law concerning unlawful sexual relations (Leviticus 18:3, 9, and 29). There shouldn't be any wrestling over a matter when you know what is right, and you definitely shouldn't make yourself sick over finding a different solution. Nonetheless, Amnon's heart was full of himself and what he wanted. The wheels were turning. In 2 Samuel 13:6, we see that Amnon pretended to be sick. Tamar prepared a meal for him. While alone with Tamar, Amnon grabbed her and said, "Come to bed with me, my sister." Tamar pleaded with him:

"No, brother!" she said, "Don't hurt me! This kind of thing isn't done in Israel! Don't do this terrible thing! Where could I ever show my face? And you — you'll be out on the street in disgrace. Oh, please! Speak to the king — he'll let you marry me."
-2 Samuel 13:12-13 MSG

Amnon refused to listen. He raped her. As a result, not only did he sin against God, but an overwhelming feeling of hate came upon him toward the very sister he fought so fiercely to abuse:

No sooner had Amnon raped her than he hated her — an immense hatred. The hatred that he felt for her was greater than the love he'd had for her. "Get up," he said, "and get out!"
-2 Samuel 13:15 MSG

Wait. Is this the same Amnon who said he was in love with Tamar and made himself sick? And now he hates her after getting what he was sick over? Something is very wrong with Amnon's heart.

Tamar, broken and hurt, pleaded and begged to stay. She told Amnon that sending her away would be a greater wrong than what he had already done to her (2 Samuel 13:16). You see, the consequences of not being a virgin in those days are nothing like today. Even a woman who had been raped was deemed unmarriageable. Unfortunately, Tamar was still sent away disgraced and ashamed. She then put ashes on her head, tore the robe that the king's virgin daughters wore, and wept loudly.

Absalom, Tamar's brother, figured out what happened. He told her, "…let's keep it quiet — a family matter…Don't take this so hard" (2 Samuel 13:20 MSG). She was then taken to Absalom's house and lived "a desolate woman". She is called "a desolate and bitter woman" in the Message Bible. Desolate is described as deserted, joyless, disconsolate, barren, lifeless. Tamar may have never recovered after being raped. Can you imagine the state of Tamar's heart? No longer was she to wear the robe that the king's virgin daughters wore. Her innocence was stolen. She was violated. How could she not take this thing to heart? Amnon ruined her life. Tamar's pain was physical and emotional. Oh, the shame, the secret she would live with for the rest of her life.

Eventually, King David received word of Tamar's rape. He was furious just like any father should be when his daughter is violated (2 Samuel 13:21). However, it doesn't appear that David addressed the matter to Amnon or Tamar. We see in scripture that he did nothing – not so much as an inquiry to see if a crime had been committed. David knew the penalty for rape under the law. He failed as a king and as a father.

I've always had questions when reading this story. Would it have been different if someone else raped Tamar besides Amnon? Was Amnon exempt from the law because he was David's son? Did David not value his daughter? I'm not advocating revenge or violence, but the fathers I know would have handled the matter somewhat differently than David. What would have happened to the perpetrator probably would have been reported on the local or national news. What would you have done if Tamar was your daughter? Or, how would your heart feel if you were Tamar, your father didn't do a thing, your rapist was free, and life was business as usual? Would you even feel safe anymore?

I'm not the only one who felt something should have been done. Absalom didn't like it. His heart was overflowing with anger. He hated Amnon and never said a word to him, neither good nor bad. The condition of Absalom's heart was about to be revealed, but Absalom's answer to revenge became a part of an unfortunate cycle.

Amnon plotted to get Tamar to his house by pretending to

be sick. Absalom plots to get Amnon to his house two years later. He waited for the perfect opportunity.

Absalom ordered his men, "Listen! When Amnon is in high spirits from drinking wine and I say to you, 'Strike Amnon down,' then kill him. Don't be afraid. Haven't I given you this order? Be strong and brave." So Absalom's men did to Amnon what Absalom had ordered. Then all the king's sons got up, mounted their mules and fled.
- 2 Samuel 13:28-29

Not only was Tamar affected by Amnon's action and David's inaction, but Absalom as well. Absalom's hate ran deep and it appeared that he had some other unresolved heart issues. There's another story about how Absalom tried to win the hearts of the people so that he could eventually take the throne away from his father (2 Samuel 15:1-6).

The situation of Amnon, King David, Tamar, and Absalom is no different than what we see in today's society. Behind closed doors, with sealed mouths, sexual violence occurs. According to the Centers for Disease Control and Prevention, sexual violence:

"is a serious public health problem in the United States that has profound impact on lifelong health, opportunity, and well-being. Sexual violence impacts every community and affects people of all genders, sexual orientations, and ages. Anyone can experience or perpetrate sexual violence. The perpetrator of sexual violence is usually someone the victim knows, such as a friend, current or former intimate partner, coworker, neighbor, or family member. …Researchers know that the numbers underestimate this problem because many cases are unreported. Victims may be ashamed, embarrassed, or afraid to tell the police, friends, or family about the violence. Victims may also keep quiet because they have been threatened with further harm if they tell anyone or do not think that anyone will help them."[5]

Just as with Tamar, sexual violence that occurs among some family members today may fall under the statement that "what goes on in this house, stays in this house." The secrets are kept and lives are affected in a very poor manner. Some have – and continue to be – taunted by them. These secrets can have lasting, harmful effects on victims and their family, friends, and communities. As a volunteer in the community, I've heard story after story from those who have been violated. They tell of feeling guilty, alone, and how the trauma leads to other things. I can relate. I, too, was a victim of sexual violence who carried the trauma even after marriage.

You may be one of those persons affected by sexual abuse, as well. There may even be those, like King David, who were aware and did nothing. You don't have to carry the burden of shame or guilt any longer. Come to Him and find rest.

"Come to me, all you who are weary and burdened, and I will give you rest. Take my yoke upon you and learn from me, for I am gentle and humble in heart, and you will find rest for your souls. For my yoke is easy and my burden is light."
-Matthew 11:28-30

Listen, don't be like the Israelites:

to whom he said, "This is the resting place, let the weary rest"; and, "This is the place of repose" – but they would not listen.
-Isaiah 28:12

It's time for you to rest. But first, let's check your heart.

YOUR HEART CONDITION

What is your heart's condition? Is there any blockage? It's time for a heart check-up. Examine and see if you recognize your heart in any of the following spiritual heart conditions:

Check	Heart Condition	Code
	Arrogant and Proud	2 Chronicles 25:19; 32:25, 26
	Discerning	Proverbs 15:14
	Turned away (from God)	1 Kings 11:3,4, 9; Isaiah 29:13
	Hardened	2 Chronicles 36:13; Isaiah 63:17; Hebrews 3:8,15; 4:7
	Stubborn	Psalm 81:12
	Deceitful	Jeremiah 17:9
	Faithless	Proverbs 14:14
	Pure	Psalm 51:10
	Fear the Lord	Deuteronomy 5:29
	Happy or cheerful	Proverbs 15:13; 17:22
	At peace	Proverbs 14:30

Based on the number of factors that you checked, what is your heart's final diagnosis? Do you need further treatment?

Our heart is vitally important to our well-being and to our lives. We must guard it to make sure it functions properly. Remember, the LORD searches the heart and examines the mind in order to "reward each person according to their conduct, according to what their deeds deserve" (Jeremiah 17:10). We guard and keep our heart flowing as we continuously submit to the leading of the Lord and follow His instructions:

My son, pay attention to what I say; turn your ear to my words. Do not let them out of your sight, keep them within your heart; for they are life to those who find them and health to one's whole body.
-Proverbs 4:20-22

Did you notice where His words are to be kept? Within our heart. Proverbs 4:20-23 (MSG) says:

Dear friend, listen well to my words; tune your ears to my voice. Keep my message in plain view at all times. Concentrate! Learn it by heart! Those who discover these words live, really live; body and soul, they're bursting with health. Keep vigilant watch over your heart; that's where life starts.

As you monitor your heart, never give up hope that things can be better. Never believe that you are beyond the reach of His love. Allow Him to face the doors with you. Open the door of your heart and let Him in. He wants you to be free so you can experience your best life. Do you sense the Lord knocking at your heart? Come on, let Him in. Your heart would love it!

DOORS WITHIN

Doors within are those doors inside the outer doors. It is behind these doors that we feel comfortable and we let our hair and guard down. No enemies are allowed. This entry and exit is for those we trust like family and friends. It's the place where we feel safest.

Joseph felt safe behind the family doors when he told his brothers his dream of having authority over them. However, he would soon be faced with the reality that the doors within were not as safe as he thought. Behind those doors were brothers with plans of killing him.

What crime had Joseph committed that demanded death or being sold into slavery? Yet, his brothers were the enemies he did not see coming. Joseph isn't the first person that dealt with doors from within. The psalmist said:

If an enemy were insulting me, I could endure it; if a foe were rising against me, I could hide. But it is you, a man like myself, my companion, my close friend, with whom I once enjoyed sweet fellowship at the house of God, as we walked about among the worshipers.
-Psalm 55:12-14

It was a trusted friend who betrayed the psalmist – one in whom he had reason to trust. The psalmist claims that a known enemy could not have had such an effect on him, but because the person was his friend, the psalmist's guard was down.

Jesus was betrayed by one of his disciples, Judas Iscariot. Before the Last Supper, Judas went to the chief priests and agreed to hand Jesus over in exchange for 30 pieces of silver. Jesus was then arrested in Gethsemane, where Judas revealed

Jesus' identity to the soldiers by giving him a kiss (Matthew 26:14-16, 47-49).

We would expect family to be our safe place but that is not always the case. Look at the division and abuse within many families. How often do we see or hear of parents and children against each other? Sometimes, there have been cases where feuding escalated to killing within the family. This is not the way it is supposed to be. Parents are supposed to love and protect their children. Children are to honor and respect their parents. The doors within what it is and what we expect are two different things.

Would you agree that betrayal from within has a different effect on your heart? It's as if you're blindsided. Imagine being in a courtroom and the prosecutor uses testimony from someone you know against you. Imagine how you would feel if you didn't see it coming.

Pause Break – Pause Break!

Have you ever experienced betrayal by a loved one or close friend? How did it make you feel? How did you handle the situation, and how did you deal with the person?

Although Joseph did not foresee the doors from within coming against him, the Lord used them for his good. And He will do the same for ours. Let's look at others who experienced some doors from within.

ESTHER, HAMAN, AND MORDECAI'S DOOR

Have you heard of Esther, Haman, or Mordecai in the Book of Esther? As we learn more about their story, you'll again see God's hand work what was meant for evil for good. Here's a little background on them: Mordecai is a Jew of the tribe of

Benjamin. He was carried into exile from Jerusalem by Nebuchadnezzar, king of Babylon. Esther is Mordecai's cousin. He raised her as his own daughter when her father and mother died. Esther later became King Xerxes' wife. Haman served in a high position in the king's court. He was elevated by King Xerxes and given a seat of honor higher than that of all the other nobles, but Mordecai did not give Haman the honor he thought he deserved (Esther 3:1, 2).

As a result of the perceived dishonor, Haman was fit to be tied. In other words, he was angry with a capital "A". Thus, Haman plotted from behind closed doors (within) to destroy Mordecai and all the Jews throughout the whole kingdom of Xerxes. He even selected a day and month: the 12th month, the month of Adar (Esther 3:3-7).

Haman told the king that the Jews did not obey the king's laws and that it wasn't in the king's best interest to tolerate them. Haman persuades the king to issue a decree for the destruction of the Jewish people on a certain day. The news spread.

However, while Haman was plotting, God had already set the stage. Mordecai made Queen Esther, who was herself a Jew, aware of the situation. She invited Haman and the king to two banquets. Haman didn't bank on the king having a dream in the middle of the night. Check this out:

That night the king could not sleep; so he ordered the book of the chronicles, the record of his reign, to be brought in and read to him. It was found recorded there that Mordecai had exposed Bigthana and Teresh, two of the king's officers who guarded the doorway, who had conspired to assassinate King Xerxes. "What honor and recognition has Mordecai received for this?" the king asked. "Nothing has been done for him," his attendants answered. The king said, "Who is in the court?" ...
-Esther 6:1-4

Guess who had just entered the outer court of the king's palace? If you guessed Haman, you were right. The king summoned him to come in. He asked him, "What should be done for the man the king delights to honor?" Haman thought the king was talking about him. Boy, was he in for a surprise. Look at Haman's response:

"...For the man the king delights to honor, have them bring a royal robe the king has worn and a horse the king has ridden, one with a royal crest placed on its head. Then let the robe and horse be entrusted to one of the king's most noble princes. Let them robe the man the king delights to honor, and lead him on the horse through the city streets, proclaiming before him, 'This is what is done for the man the king delights to honor!'"
-Esther 6:7-9

Now, look at the details of Haman's response. He's a smooth operator. Unlike Joseph when he spoke to Pharaoh, Haman's thought was of himself. The king liked Haman's suggestion and told him to go immediately and do as he suggested for Mordecai. The king even told him to not neglect anything Haman recommended. Can you imagine Haman's face? I picture Haman picking up his face from the floor. After picking it up, he did as the king instructed:

So Haman got the robe and the horse. He robed Mordecai, and led him on horseback through the city streets, proclaiming before him, "This is what is done for the man the king delights to honor!"
-Esther 6:11

Can you imagine the excitement in Haman's voice as he leads Mordecai on horseback through the city? I'm just kidding. Haman rushed home with his head covered in grief when he was finished (Esther 6:12). The plot thickens when it comes time for Haman to attend the banquet prepared by Queen Esther.

The king and Haman both attended Queen Esther's banquet. The king asked, "Queen Esther, what is your petition? It will be given you. What is your request? Even up to half the kingdom, it will be granted." Queen Esther informed the king of the plot to kill her and the other Jews. "Who is he? Where is he — the man who has dared to do such a thing?" King Xerxes asked (Esther 7:1-5).

"An adversary and enemy! This vile Haman!" Esther said (Esther 7:6).

Can you picture Haman picking up his face again? And this time, he might even find his heart there, too.

Esther's revelation of Haman enrages the king, who was further angered when (after leaving the room briefly and returning) he discovered Haman had fallen on Esther's couch, intending to beg for mercy from Esther. The king interpreted this as a sexual advance (Esther 7:8).

As a result of his intentions, Haman was executed on gallows that he had erected for Mordecai. Jews throughout the empire were permitted to defend themselves on the day set for their extermination. And, Mordecai became the king's chief advisor (Esther 8:2).

See, the evil Haman planned against the Jews behind those doors turned out for good. Were you able to see the hand of God in this story? Do you think it was a coincidence that the king had a dream about an incident that occurred in the past? I don't think so. God had a plan the whole time and it didn't include killing off His people. Guess what? He feels the same way about you.

We have used several examples of doors in the Bible to show what they are and how God uses them. Now, we're going to switch gears to discuss some real-life doors within that people have experienced. Names have been changed, and these are only snapshots of their lives, but the reality of these doors can likely relate to experiences that any of us have had. Let's watch how God moves in the lives of these individuals, in their own words.

SALLY'S DOOR

My husband, Joe, and I have been happily married for 20 years. We have two sons. One day, Joe came home holding the hand of a 5-year-old girl.

"Daddy, Daddy", the little girl said.

"Why is she calling you Daddy, Joe? Whose child is that?" I asked.

"She's mine," Joe said.

"Yours!"

"Her mother was arrested. They called me to pick her up. She had nowhere else to go."

I felt like my heart was about to faint as it raced past its speed limit. Here was my husband, the man I loved, standing in our home with a child that he had kept a secret for five entire years. This had been a secret not only from me, but our sons, too. I would later find out that Joe's mother and siblings knew all about the child the whole time. They had frequent visits with her. Joe's family and I were close, so I thought. But they had kept this secret.

This was a hard pill to swallow. I was faced with infidelity, hurt, pain, and deception. I also felt some kind of way toward Joe's family. I actually thought they loved me, but if that was the case, I couldn't understand how love could have kept the child a secret. They were in my face. We ate and took trips together. We were family.

Surviving infidelity is difficult all by itself, but to add to that an innocent child born outside of the marriage was picture perfect for Divorce Court. So many questions raced through my mind. I wondered about our sons. How would they react when they learned their father cheated on me and had another child? How would this affect them?

My heart was hurting but I still loved Joe. I thought about divorcing him. I would cry every time I thought about what I was going through. I had been betrayed by the one who said, "I will love you till death do us part. I will have no others before you." I even wondered if I had done something wrong to cause him to go outside our marriage to another woman. I found myself getting mad all over again as I thought about the risk Joe put me in of catching a disease by him messing around. What if I had caught AIDS?

I felt like I was losing it and needed to talk to someone, so I called a dear friend. I shared with her what happened. She was non-judgmental and asked me one question that stuck with me. She asked, "Do you love him?" I told her I did. We continued to talk. I left in better spirits thinking about the things we discussed. But I was still hurting. I took my marriage vows seriously. I came from a long family line of failed marriages. I decided that when I got married that my marriage would last. So, I decided I wanted our marriage to work.

Although I wanted our marriage to survive, it was hard to even look at Joe when he initially tried talking to me. I was hurting. He and I talked later when I settled down. He apologized for everything and told me he wanted our marriage to work, too. I expressed how hurt I was and told him I didn't know if I could trust him like I did before. He said he understood and was willing to do whatever it took to regain my trust. We knew it wasn't going to be a smooth walk in the park. We committed our marriage to the Lord and went to marriage counseling. We continued to work through the matter of his child. She was innocent and deserved to have a good life.

It's been years since then, but I still have some days where I start to feel a certain kind of way about the past. I'm still working through that. Thoughts come across my mind and I am able to freely talk to Joe about them. We love one another and continue to be committed to our marriage. The truth is that it has made us stronger. Joe and I are closer than ever before, and we've used our story to encourage and help others. What was meant to destroy our marriage – and what was meant to destroy *me* – turned out for good.

JAMES' DOOR

There is a huge difference between discipline and abuse. I know because as a child, I've seen and experienced both. This is my example of discipline: you are fighting over a toy in a room with your brother or a sister. Your parent comes in, sees it, and spanks or pops you on the butt. You're told that you're not supposed to do that and sent to another room to think about what you did.

My example of abuse, using the same situation, is when your parent's response is out of control. It's wrong when a child does nothing and a parent takes frustration out on the child because the parent had a bad day. The child didn't ask to come into this world. The child is helpless and relies on the parent. Parents are supposed to be their children's protector.

I remember my dad coming home one day. My brother and I had been rowdy, aggravating my mom and each other. I guess my dad had a bad day. He took some plastic grocery bags and tied them over our heads as he rambled on about us being kings. I put a hole in the bag over my head so I could breathe.

My brother almost passed out but my mom saved him. My dad turned around and took his anger out on her. Even today, my dad will not admit that he did that to us. I never let it bother me to the point that I want to get angry anymore, but I'm continuously trying to learn from it to make sure I don't make the same mistakes. My brother spent his whole life trying to forget about it. It affected him and he stayed in trouble the first part of his life. He's fine now.

My best memories of my childhood are of my mother. She was never abusive or physically abused us like my dad. Mom was always the one taking the brunt of the abuse for us. I have a better understanding of a mother's love. I don't mean that there is no such thing as a father's love because all fathers aren't like mine. He, too, experienced abuse as a child. He told us how his mom would wake him up and beat him with a baseball bat.

This was still no excuse to treat us like he did, but hopefully it paints a subtle picture of cycles of abuse that are unattended.

I've forgiven him. I never wanted to be like him. I've never treated women like he did my mom. I've never had children of my own. There's a part of me that was scared. I was afraid I would make the same mistakes as my dad did. But now I don't believe that anymore. I would never abuse any child. I know what it feels like and how it affects you.

My life, as a child, wasn't easy. I am grateful to the people who picked us up for church. The church was a safe place. We knew we wouldn't be hurt there. Honestly, I tried to deny that there was a God when I became a teenager. I've had my run-ins with disbelief. But I know there has to be a God up there. I recognize that I could have never survived without Him.

LISA'S DOOR

I was pregnant at the age of 16. The father of my child and I married. I soon found out that he was an addict. He wouldn't keep a job. I would hide my money because he wanted it for his drug addiction. I was beaten badly with a broom when I was pregnant with my second child. This resulted in me being placed on bed rest. I didn't tell my mom. I just cried all the time. I felt all alone.

For the next six years, I dealt with abuse and infidelity in our marriage. He fathered an outside child. We were on and off. One night I had a dream. I saw my deceased grandmother. She said, "Baby, I want you to leave. This man is going to kill you or you are going to kill him. You leave now." This was the straw that broke the camel's back. I finally left him. I left with my boys and three baskets of clothes.

He stalked and harassed me wherever he could find me, including at my job. Security would escort me to my vehicle. He wouldn't leave me alone even when I moved in with my mom. Then, one day I was out with a friend. Our sons were with my ex-husband. They called out to me and I went to see what they wanted. I turned my back to leave and my ex-husband hit me in the head with some object. I fell to the ground, where he kicked me all over my body.

He then fled the scene. The ambulance and police were called. The cover was pulled on me as I was transported by ambulance to the hospital. I would later learn that my children were crying because someone told them I was dead. I was released from the hospital, swollen, with a fractured jaw and collar bone. Days followed where I would scream and holler all night from the trauma of what happened to me.

The police searched but could not find him. He eventually turned himself in and appeared in court. The judge told him if he ever did anything else, he would do time for the crime he had done. That didn't stop him. He still tried.

I decided to protect myself and took a friend's gun without his knowledge. I planned to kill him before he hurt me again. My mom heard that I had the gun and asked me an important question, "What will happen to your boys?" This made me think, so I returned the gun. My uncle came to town. He went to see my ex-husband. He said, "I heard you like whipping on women." My uncle gave him a good whipping. That day sealed it and he never bothered me again.

This door shattered me when it came to men. I didn't want to date anyone because of what I'd experienced. I wasn't going through that again.

Fast forward years later, my ex-husband – the man who abused, beat, and cheated on me – needed a place to recover after surgery. I allowed him to stay in our guest room with my younger son and me during that time.

I have been able to help others with what I've been through. I tell young women that they should not allow men to abuse them. Instead, they should be treated and respected like a queen.

What was meant to hurt me is being used for good. I am no longer the same. I am safe and I am free. To God be the glory. God did it for me and he can do the same thing for you too.

MANY DOORS FROM WITHIN

No one plans or expects to be betrayed from within. It's our safe place. Yet, we face these doors all the time: abuse, drug addiction of a child or parent, infidelity, spousal abuse, heartaches, disappointments, haters, and others. Then we're faced with the choices of how to deal with them. Some of these are more traumatic and cause us to struggle in life. In the betrayals, we feel helpless. We can't understand why. It hurts. We try to make sense out of it and may even believe it's our fault. We may look at others differently and question their intentions. After all, we've been betrayed and our trust antenna stays up.

I've never understood why a person would abuse someone they love. As a child, I've heard the wife next door scream, "Larry, Larry, stop. Larry, stop!" as he was beating her like an ole' master would a slave. I wanted her to run away so he would stop beating her. I vowed to myself that it wasn't going to be that way for me. My husband shares my feelings. His words to the young man who asked for our daughter's hand in marriage were, "Don't put your hands on her". He's a man of few words but he meant every word he spoke.

Seek help if you find yourself in an abusive relationship. You are a child of the King and deserve better. There are some resources in the back of this book that can direct you to help in your area. Again, if you are in danger, seek immediate help. Remember, you are not alone.

You don't have to be weighed down or held hostage at these doors any longer. You've been there long enough. You've been set free. You are not alone. Joseph's doors remind us that God will be with us and is always faithful regardless of what we face. As He was with Joseph, He will be with you. You only have to look to Him.

God can and is willing to keep you safe within the doors. It's time to be healed and move on from the scars and memories. You no longer have to be enslaved. Are you ready to be free?

The Lord will allow you to use your experiences with doors within to encourage others, just like those in this book. Isn't that just like Him to take what was meant to destroy or kill you, and use it for our benefit?

DOORS OF UNFORGIVENESS

Unforgiveness is one of those hot topics. If there was a top ten list for doors we face in life, unforgiveness would probably be number two. We've seen it and have probably experienced it. We've probably said:

"I will never forgive him"
"I will never forgive her"
"How could we forgive them after all they've done?"
"It will be a cold day in hell before I......."
"That xxxxx. I tell you xxxx...."

You get the picture. Our emotions are everywhere when we face this door. Forgiveness is likely the last thing on our minds. In fact, most of us are on the complete opposite end of forgiveness. We want revenge. We want the person who wronged us to suffer. After all, they need to pay. However, a child's point of view differs a little from adults. Check out these perspectives after a brief interview with some children:

Brooklyn (6 years old):
What does forgiveness mean? You say I'm sorry and I forgive you.
What if they don't say I'm sorry? I would say sorry back to them.
Why? Because they didn't say sorry.
Has anyone ever done something to you but you hadn't done anything to them? One time my little sister kept hitting me until I told my dad.
Did you play with her anymore? Yes!

Anna (6 years old):
What is forgiveness? You say you sorry.

How would you feel if I hit you for no reason? I would feel sad. Then I'll tell somebody.

Would you like me anymore? I wouldn't like you.

What if I came to you and said I'm sorry? You would have to do something for me.

Cooper (6 years old):

What is forgiveness? That means you share with people.

What if someone hit you and you hadn't done anything to them? I will go tell.

What if the person said they were sorry? I will say I forgive you and I won't tell on them.

What if they don't say they're sorry? I will tell on them.

Would you forgive them even if they don't say I'm sorry? Yes, Ma'am. Did I get all the answers right?

Landon (8 years old):

What is forgiveness? To help somebody.

How would you feel if someone did something bad to you? I would feel sad.

Would you do something back to them? I wouldn't do anything to them.

What if they say they were sorry? I would say it's okay. We'll still play and be friends.

What if you did something wrong to your brother? I would apologize. I would tell him I'm sorry because I did the wrong thing.

Ah'Kenleigh (6 years old):

What does it mean to forgive somebody? Sorry.

How would you feel if someone did something bad to you and did not say they were sorry? Sad.

How would you treat them? Very nice.

Why? So, they can be nice back to me.

What would you do if you did something wrong to someone? I would say sorry. I'm so sorry.

Maybe we need a childlike approach when it comes to forgiveness. We can surely learn from them.

For most people, a forgiving response doesn't come naturally. Forgiving others, and ourselves, seems to be one of the hardest things some of us ever have to do. Why? All people make mistakes and sin. God forgives them. People are acting in a godlike manner when they forgive.

At times it is difficult to face the wrongs that have been done to us. Sometimes we deny – even to ourselves – the severity of our wounds. In other cases, we are well aware of the hurts we've experienced, and we believe the person should suffer some consequences for what he or she did. If we forgive, it seems we're letting the person off too easily.

You may carry memories of hurt and pain from some of the doors you have encountered. Your parents may have rejected or abused you (physically or mentally). Perhaps your mother preferred your sister because your mom felt your sister was smart and you were not. Or maybe your father made it his habit to hit you first and ask questions later. You might even be in a relationship that requires you to forgive every day.

Life offers us plenty of opportunities to feel unforgiving. The trouble is, lack of forgiveness does more damage to us than to the one who wronged us. When we don't forgive, we grow hardened, untrusting, sour, or bitter.

Notice in the story of Joseph that his brothers were afraid that he would hold a grudge against them and pay them back for all the wrong they did to him. Remember, they sent word to Joseph saying, "Your father left these instructions before he died: 'This is what you are to say to Joseph: I ask you to forgive your brothers the sins and the wrongs they committed in treating you so badly.' Now please forgive the sins of the servants of the God of your father" (Genesis 50:16-17). Instead of revenge, Joseph wept when he received their message.

It seemed that he had no problem letting them off the hook, so to speak. He was in charge and could have used his authority to get even with them. Had he forgotten how they treated him when they sold him into slavery? Maybe he had moved from that door. I'm not sure how I would have responded. I would like to think (*like* to think, I said) I could have responded like Joseph, but I am still not sure. I'm still on the potter's wheel and He's still working on me. We don't always know how we would respond until it's right in our face and we have to make a decision.

Joseph seems to have guarded his heart. And we should, too. We should forgive those who have treated us wrong. That includes forgiving ourselves when we've failed and need to be forgiven.

FORGIVE FOR YOUR SAKE

Unless you're perfect, you have done things that need to be forgiven (even if no one else knows about them but God). Do you want to be forgiven? Then, it is for your good to forgive others. There's no way around it. It's written:

For if you forgive other people when they sin against you, your heavenly Father will also forgive you. But if you do not forgive others their sins, your Father will not forgive your sins.
-Matthew 6:14-15

Do you pray? Do you want your prayers answered? It's written:

And when you stand praying, if you hold anything against anyone, forgive them, so that your Father in heaven may forgive you your sins."
-Mark 11:25

Are you one of God's chosen ones? It's written:

Therefore, as God's chosen people, holy and dearly loved, clothe yourselves with compassion, kindness, humility, gentleness and patience. Bear with each other and forgive one another if any of you has a grievance against someone. Forgive as the Lord forgave you.
-Colossians 3:12-13

Again, there's no way around it. We must forgive. Don't allow unforgiveness to keep you trapped behind its door.

I'm not an expert on forgiveness. I forgive because I read the Word and I understand the benefits of it. I've done things in my life that I'm not proud of and have experienced forgiveness from God, others, and myself. I'm not perfect like those who feel they've done no wrong and don't need forgiveness or feel the need to forgive. The truth is they're fooling themselves and need to break out of that door. They're locked in, being robbed, and don't even realize it.

The scripture tells us that God so loved the world that He sent His one and only son, Jesus (John 3:16). Then Jesus willingly gave up His life: His blood was shed on the cross to provide forgiveness for our sins (Romans 5:8-9, Hebrews 5:8-9). Oh, how they love us. And we're told to love one another. In loving each other, we forgive others as He did us (in our sinful state). We have all sinned against each other and God. Yet, He chooses to freely forgive us when we repent. The truth is that He let us off the hook. We should extend it to others. Even those who didn't seem sorry or never said they were wrong have access to forgiveness. Romans 5:8 says, "But God demonstrates his own love for us in this: While we were still sinners, Christ died for us."

Look at this parable that Jesus shared of the Unmerciful Servant in Matthew 18:21-35:

Then Peter came to Jesus and asked, "Lord, how many times shall I forgive my brother or sister who sins against me? Up to seven times?" Jesus answered, "I tell you, not seven times, but seventy-seven times. "Therefore, the kingdom of heaven is like a king who wanted to settle accounts with his servants. As he began the settlement, a man who owed him ten thousand bags of gold was brought to him. Since he was not able to pay, the master ordered that he and his wife and his children and all that he had be sold to repay the debt. "At this the servant fell on his knees before him. 'Be patient with me,' he begged, 'and I will pay back everything.' The servant's master took pity on him, canceled the debt and let him go. "But when that servant went out, he found one of his fellow servants who owed him a hundred silver coins. He grabbed him and began to choke him. 'Pay back what you owe me!' he demanded. "His fellow servant fell to his knees and begged him, 'Be patient with me, and I will pay it back.'

"But he refused. Instead, he went off and had the man thrown into prison until he could pay the debt. When the other servants saw what had happened, they were outraged and went and told their master everything that had happened. "Then the master called the servant in. 'You wicked servant,' he said, 'I canceled all that debt of yours because you begged me to. Shouldn't you have had mercy on your fellow servant just as I had on you?' In anger his master handed him over to the jailers to be tortured, until he should pay back all he owed. "This is how my heavenly Father will treat each of you unless you forgive your brother or sister from your heart."

How do you see yourself in this parable? Are you willing to forgive?

Pause Break – Pause Break!

We don't know if Joseph's brothers truly felt sorry for what they had done to Joseph. They didn't seem to have any problem selling Joseph off as a slave. Do you think it mattered to Joseph by the time they were before him? How is Joseph able to speak kindly to them after what they did to him? How have you responded when you've been wronged and others asked to be forgiven? What stands in the balance when you don't forgive others? Is it worth it?

Unforgiveness is like a cancer that will eat away at you until you are consumed from within. It will rot you to the bones. Is it worth having cancer to you? Remember: you don't forgive for his or her sake. You forgive them for your sake.

FORGIVE FOR YOUR HEALTH'S SAKE

Forgiveness is not just a matter of spiritual healing. It affects your mental and physical health. Research suggests that forgiveness can benefit people's health.

John Hopkins' studies have found that the act of forgiveness can reap huge rewards for your health, such as the following: lowering the risk of heart attack; improving cholesterol levels and sleep; and reducing pain, blood pressure, and levels of anxiety, depression and stress. Chronic anger puts you into a fight-or-flight mode, which results in numerous changes in heart rate, blood pressure and immune response. Those changes, then, increase the risk of depression, heart disease and diabetes, among other conditions. Forgiveness, however, calms stress levels, leading to improved health.[6]

I read about Dr. Everett Worthington, Commonwealth Professor Emeritus, who studied forgiveness. His research was put to the test: his mother was murdered in a home invasion. He tells how knowing Jesus made all the difference in forgiving the man who murdered his mom. He said:

"Trying to forgive my mom's killers was like standing in a storm on top of Mount LeConte. My instinct was to huddle down in pain. But that personal relationship with Jesus that had transformed me at the youth conference set me on a different path. ... Through prayer, I could see the young man's fear of prison and anger at having his plans spoiled. Being able to empathize with him didn't mean I accepted what he had done. But it did help me forgive him."[7]

When Worthington and his siblings were asked if forgiving the murderer dishonored their mother, they said, "Mama taught us to forgive. It would dishonor her if we didn't forgive."

Forgiveness doesn't mean you're not holding people accountable for their actions. You're not letting someone off the hook of their prison term or the fact that you don't think they did the right thing. You're making a choice and letting yourself off the hook for your health's sake. Picture this with me:

Symptom: Depression   **Diagnosis**: Unforgiveness
Symptom: Arthritis   **Diagnosis**: Unforgiveness
Symptom: Blood Pressure   **Diagnosis**: Unforgiveness

One study spoke of how people felt angry and stressed when they recalled a wrong against them. I can relate. Somewhere around the age of 13 or 14, my great-grandmother, Grandma Susie, came to our house. Grandma Susie had been drinking. She was angry, said some horrible things, and called us everything except a child of God. You wouldn't expect a grandmother to say what she said to her grandchild. She had her long switch and was there to whip my (expletive), she said. The neighbor telephoned Momma (that's what I call my grandmother). Momma is Grandma Susie's daughter. Momma told Grandma Susie that she was not going to let her whip me. Grandma Susie responded that she was going to whip Momma if she didn't get out of the way.

I can remember Momma saying, "Ma, well you'll have to whip me". I have to be honest: I had no plans of getting a whipping because if she had come through those doors, I would have shot her with my mom's gun. That sounds horrible, I know, but it happened. In case you're wondering, let me tell you – in two sentences – how it started. *My little brother, Phillip, called wanting to come home because Grandma Susie was drunk. I went and brought him home.* That's it.

The relationship and how I felt about Grandma Susie were never the same after that day and life just went on. I tried to avoid every interaction with her. There was never any discussion about the incident. After all, she was an adult and we were children. I never forgot what she said and carried it into my adult life. The truth is I *tolerated* her.

Fred and I married and had our firstborn. My mom was excited and hesitantly asked if she could take her firstborn grandchild to see Grandma Susie. My immediate response was 'no' but I allowed my mom to take her with the understanding that if "Grandma Susie say anything about or treat my baby any kind of way that she would never see her again." I had held on to those horrible words Grandma Susie spoke. You know what else? She never asked us to forgive her, and it wasn't until while writing this section of the book that I realized I needed to forgive her (even if she's deceased). I said out loud, "I forgive you, Grandma Susie". I let it go for *me*, and I can't explain the feeling.

Are you holding on to wrongs toward you, even if the person didn't apologize? Do you allow life to go on as if it never happened? It's time to face/address/deal with it. I recommend to you, too: let it go. It's for YOU.

Will you allow those who hurt you to rob you of your psychological well-being and physical health? It's your choice.

FORGIVENESS IS A CHOICE

Forgiveness can seem like a beast at times, but it is a beast that can be conquered. No one can force it on you, not even God. It is your God-given, inalienable right to forgive someone who hurts you. It can't be taken or given away or transferred to another person. Just as Joseph, only you can make the choice.

On June 17, 2015, national news reported that nine people were murdered while attending their Wednesday night Bible Study in Charleston, North Carolina. The parishioners had welcomed their killer, Dylan Roof, into their group, not knowing his intentions.[8] One can only imagine the grief and pain felt by their families at the news of their loved ones' deaths.

Yet, on June 19, 2015, the world would see and hear from victims' relatives who spoke at a bond hearing for the accused.[9]

"I forgive you. You took something very precious from me. I will never talk to her again. I will never, ever hold her again. But I forgive you. And have mercy on your soul."

"I forgive you. You took something very precious away from me. I will never get to talk to her ever again. I will never be able to hold her again, but I forgive you, and have mercy on your soul. ... You hurt me. You hurt a lot of people. If God forgives you, I forgive you."

"I would just like him to know that, to say the same thing that was just said: I forgive him and my family forgives him. But we would like him to take this opportunity to repent. Repent. Confess. Give your life to the one who matters most: Christ. So that He can change him and change your ways, so no matter what happens to you, and you'll be okay."

"We welcomed you Wednesday night in our Bible study with open arms. You have killed some of the most beautiful people that I know. Every fiber in my body hurts and I'll, I'll never be the same. ... May God have mercy on you."

"Although my grandfather and the other victims died at the hands of hate, this is proof, everyone's plea for your soul, is proof that they lived in love and their legacies will live in love. So hate won't win. And I just want to thank the court for making sure that hate doesn't win."

"That was my sister, and I'd like to thank you on behalf of my family for not allowing hate to win. For me, I'm a work in progress. And I acknowledge that I am very angry. ... We have no room for hating, so we have to forgive. I pray God on your soul."

You see, none of the family members returned anger, even as the accused looked as if he wasn't remorseful. They offered him forgiveness and said they were praying for his soul, even as they described the pain of their losses. How could they forgive a young man who said, "I still feel like I had to do it"?[10] They made a choice.

On October 2, 2019, many people witnessed a young man, Brandt Jean, hugging a young lady, Amber Guyger, on national television. Brandt publicly forgave Guyger – a former Dallas police officer – who killed his older brother, Botham, in his own apartment.[11] Guyger said that she entered the apartment believing it was her own and that she shot Botham believing he was a burglar.

I feel confident that Brandt's hug shocked the world. I watched as Brandt was on the stand during the sentencing hearing. He said:

"If you truly are sorry, I can speak for myself, I forgive, and I know if you go to God and ask him, he will forgive you."

"And I don't think anyone can say it – again I'm speaking for myself, not even for my family – but I love you just like anyone else."

"And I'm not gonna say I hope you rot and die just like my brother did, but I personally want the best for you."

"And I wasn't going to ever say this in front of my family or anyone, but I don't even want you to go to jail. I want the best for you, because I know that's exactly what Botham would want you to do."

"And the best would be give your life to Christ. I'm not going to say anything else. I think giving your life to Christ would be the best thing that Botham would want you to do."

"Again, I love you as a person and I don't wish anything bad on you."

You can see the judge as she is crying. He then turns to the Judge and says: "I don't know if this is possible, but can I give her (Guyger) a hug, please? Please?"

Presiding Judge Tammy Kemp responded, "Yes," and Brandt left the stand and hugged her. What Brandt reminded me of was Joseph's response when he revealed himself to his brothers. He acknowledged their wrong and forgave them at the same time (Genesis 50:20-21).

I would later watch in another CNN video Brandt's comment that his brother's death made him angry and he pretty much hated Guyger. He worked on himself and let the anger go. Brandt said, "Forgiveness is what you have to do to set yourself free and to have peace of mind." This bears repeating: "Forgiveness is what you have to do to set yourself free and to have peace of mind." Brandt made a choice. It was his choice and evidently one that he had been pondering.

His family didn't know what he intended to say. Many on social media championed Brandt Jean as an example for all Christians to follow. Others raised concerns that his gesture might distract from the black community's cries for justice in police shooting cases. How others viewed it made no difference.[12] Brandt serves as a reminder that forgiveness is not about what others may feel. It's about *you*, the one doing the forgiving. Remember what he said, "Forgiveness is what you have to do to set yourself free and to have peace of mind."

Emotions ran high and many were crying inside the courtroom. Everyone had just witnessed the brother of the deceased hugging and forgiving the accused. Not only that. At the conclusion of the trial, we would see the response of Judge Kemp towards Guyger that day. The accused asked Judge Kemp about forgiveness and requested a Bible and a hug. The judge spoke with her about forgiveness, gave her a Bible, and a hug. Judge Kemp received support and criticism for her display of compassion toward Guyger. Judge Kemp's response was this: "As a Christian, I believe I'm commanded to offer her love and compassion just as Brandt Jean did."[13] I listened to various videos as Judge Kemp would say: "Guyger will forever be the murderer of Botham Jean. How she carries that thus forward depends on how we receive her. The act that she committed was horrific – she murdered Mr. Jean, but none of us are one thing that we've done."

That's powerful. I was encouraged and convicted on one hand as I viewed the one-on-one interview with Judge Kemp.[14] I'm so glad God isn't finished with me yet. What about you?

Many will never forget what happened in these incidents. Our hearts go out to the families involved in any tragedy. We do not have to agree with the actions of the accused or any involved, including the media. Matthew 7:12 reminds us, "So in everything, do to others what you would have them do to you...". The Message version says, "Here is a simple, rule-of-thumb guide for behavior: Ask yourself what you want people to do for you, then grab the initiative and do it for them. ..."

If you were in the wrong, what do you want people to do for you? We've all sinned. Jesus made that clear when He said, "He who is without sin cast the first stone" (John 8:7), and there was not a one who would. I don't know about you, but I can't throw a stone, and besides that, I want forgiveness.

Pause Break – Pause Break!

The topic of forgiveness can be a struggle. We will have to face the door of forgiving and being forgiven one day ourselves. Do you want to be reminded of the wrong you've done? Would you want to be forgiven? Would you hold resentment toward others? Are you concerned about what others may think if you forgive someone who is in the wrong?

We've heard many stories of those forgiving others for the wrong they have done, to include stories from those who have been wrongfully incarcerated for years, just like Joseph.

How do you forgive one parent who kills the other parent? How do you forgive when you've spent 44 years behind bars for a crime you didn't commit? It can be hard. As easy as it is to say, "Just forgive," we need to actually work at forgiving until it becomes a way of life for us.

In the Book of Hosea, the Lord had Hosea, an Old Testament prophet, marry a prostitute named Gomer. Notice, God had Hosea to do this. I don't recommend you take it upon yourself. So, Hosea took her as his wife, but Gomer was unfaithful. She kept cheating on Hosea. She left him with the kids and went out into the arms of other lovers — turning her back on him and committing adultery again and again. And yet the Lord told Hosea to keep going after her again, and to bring her back home. Every time I read this story, I think of Hosea's obedience to God. He really, really loved God. I do not think anyone would have looked down on Hosea for divorcing her. Some may have even told him to get rid of her. Would you have gone back again after a spouse continuously cheated on you? I would really have to see the handwriting on the wall, "Linda, take him back. LINDA TAKE HIM BACK", and know in my knower that it was God. As I told you earlier, God is still working on me. The fact that Hosea was obedient may also indicate that he forgave her. I believe Hosea is a picture of God's love and faithfulness to the Israelites. Time and time again, they played the adulteress role in serving other gods. God would go after them. They would repent and He forgave them. God had a choice. Hosea had a choice, and we, too, have a choice.

Luke 15 tells a story of the Prodigal Son who asks for his portion of inheritance from his father. The father gives it to him.

"Not long after that, the younger son got together all he had, set off for a distant country and there squandered his wealth in wild living. After he had spent everything, there was a severe famine in that whole country, and he began to be in need. So he went and hired himself out to a citizen of that country, who sent him to his fields to feed pigs. He longed to fill his stomach with the pods that the pigs were eating, but no one gave him anything.
-Luke 15:13-16

While in the pig pen, the son has a wake-up call:

"When he came to his senses, he said, 'How many of my father's hired servants have food to spare, and here I am starving to death! I will set out and go back to my father and say to him: Father, I have sinned against heaven and against you. I am no longer worthy to be called your son; make me like one of your hired servants.' So he got up and went to his father. "But while he was still a long way off, his father saw him and was filled with compassion for him; he ran to his son, threw his arms around him and kissed him. "The son said to him, 'Father, I have sinned against heaven and against you. I am no longer worthy to be called your son.'
-Luke 15:17-21

Look at his father's response:

"But the father said to his servants, 'Quick! Bring the best robe and put it on him. Put a ring on his finger and sandals on his feet. Bring the fattened calf and kill it. Let's have a feast and celebrate. For this son of mine was dead and is alive again; he was lost and is found.' So they began to celebrate."
-Luke 15:22-24

What a picture of forgiveness! The father didn't tell him, "You got what you deserved." Instead, he had a party. This wayward son got the best robe, a ring on his finger, and sandals on his feet. Was this the way to treat a child who recklessly used his portion of his inheritance? You know, the portion that he would receive if you were dead. Did he really get what he deserved? What do you think caused his father to respond as he did? How would you have responded if you were his father or this was your child? One last question. How would you have wanted to be treated if you were the son?

FORGIVING DOESN'T MEAN YOU FORGET

Forgiving doesn't mean forgetting, nor does it mean that you've given the approval that what someone did was OK. It just means that you've let go of the anger or guilt towards someone, or towards yourself. But that can be easier said than done. If forgiveness was easy, everyone would be doing it.

Joseph married and had two sons. Their names were a reminder and represented his experience:

Joseph named his firstborn Manasseh and said, "It is because God has made me forget all my trouble and all my father's household." The second son he named Ephraim and said, "It is because God has made me fruitful in the land of my suffering."
-Genesis 41:51-52

Wow. He says that God made him forget all his trouble and his father's household. How could he? Joseph didn't forget his trouble or his father's household in the sense that he had no memory. He identified himself to his brothers, "I am your brother Joseph, the one you sold into Egypt". Joseph also recognized God's plan in sending him ahead of his brothers to preserve for them a remnant on earth and to save their lives by a great deliverance (Genesis 45:4-7). Here's a quote that describes the "forgetting" that Joseph may have sought:

"Forgiving does not erase the bitter past. A healed memory is not a deleted memory. Instead, forgiving what we cannot forget creates a new way to remember. We change the memory of our past into a hope for our future." –Lewis B. Smedes[15]

While Joseph chose to forgive and reconcile with his brothers, know that there are some situations that don't allow for any reconciliation to occur. It takes two people to reconcile, but only one to forgive.

What kind of person would Joseph have become if he had nurtured an unforgiving spirit? Scripture gives us every piece of evidence that he didn't let injustice change his character or his trust in God. It didn't matter about his position or where he was: whether in the house of Potiphar, chained in a prison cell on a false charge of rape, or sitting on a throne in Egypt. The scriptures say God's favor was upon him: "The Lord was with Joseph and he prospered. ...The Lord gave him success in everything he did. ... The Lord was with him; he showed him kindness and granted him favor" (Genesis 39:2-6, 21).

Do you want the favor of God in your life? If so, face the door, make the choice, and forgive. If you're still not convinced that it's in your best interest to forgive, here are some more questions to ponder:

- Is unforgiveness worth your prayers not being answered and God not forgiving you?
- Is unforgiveness worth losing your health?

- Is it worth you not being blessed?
- Do you want peace of mind?

Don't allow unforgiveness to keep you imprisoned. You're not bound like a bird trapped in a cage. You're free to forgive. Forgiveness can't change the past. Forgiveness is not about the other person. It is about freedom for the one who forgives: You. Face the door, make a choice, and experience your God-given freedom. The Son came to set you free, and whom He sets free is free indeed (John 8:36).

MELANIE'S DOOR

My parents went their separate ways when I was around the age of six. My mother was left to raise us as a single parent while my daddy moved out of the state. It was difficult for my mother but she worked hard to make sure our needs were met. I remember her working two regular jobs. In addition to those two, she picked up side jobs as they came available.

We lived in several places, including government- assisted living apartments. In one set of the apartments, there lived a man named Mr. Tim. He sold candy from his apartment. All the children went there to get their fill, even the ones who didn't have any money. I was one of them.

"You want some candy?" he would ask.

"Yes, but I don't have any money," I'd respond.

"Don't worry about that. I'll give you some candy," said Mr. Tim.

Mr. Tim always waited until no one was around to give us our candy, and what came along with it should have never happened to a child. But if I wanted candy, I would have to lie on the bed and allow Mr. Tim to fondle me. As a 6-year-old, innocent child, I didn't think anything Mr. Tim did to me was wrong or illegal. There was never any conversation among the children in the community. Every child who wanted some candy went to see Mr. Tim. The children's innocence was compromised by a man who knew better. Their secrets would be carried into their adulthood.

This type of treatment didn't stop with Mr. Tim. I was around the age of 7 or 8 when I asked my grandmother to tell my mother to leave her boyfriend alone. My grandmother didn't ask any questions but she told her. I know she did because my mother came to me and said, "Momma told me what you said. She can't tell me what to do. I am grown. This is my house."

She didn't even ask why I felt that way. Neither did I tell her why I wanted her to stop her boyfriend from coming around. I didn't tell her what he had been doing to me when she left for work or wasn't around. I felt she wouldn't believe me. To me, she loved him more.

There was one adult who recognized that something was wrong. She said, "Melanie, you hate him so much. Is he messing with you?"

I didn't respond and she didn't follow up. I carried this secret into my adult life and marriage. Here is something that I find interesting, though. This particular adult who asked the question is legally blind and sensed what was going on with me. Those who had their physical sight didn't sense a thing, or at least didn't ask any questions. I was a child crying out for help.

Why didn't I tell it? I don't know. Why didn't my mother and grandmother ask any questions? Why did they not see what was going on before their very eyes?

I continued to live with this door after my marriage. I shared with my husband what occurred when I was young. I kept my daughter within my sight and would not allow her to spend nights away from home for fear that what happened to me would happen to her. I became that overprotecting mother who was on watch for every male figure who had contact with my daughter. I promised myself that it wouldn't happen to her. I even threatened to kill an uncle who married into our family and was known for inappropriately touching girls. He knew I meant every word I said. I even watched and warned my niece.

I didn't want the same thing to happen to her.

Why wouldn't children tell they are being abused, you may ask? According to Childsafe House Advocacy Center there could be many reasons. Maybe they didn't recognize what was happening to them as abuse. Children are often groomed before abuse and may think what is happening is normal. Sexual predators are master manipulators and will often tell children to keep the abuse a "secret," and that it's something special that just the two of them are doing. This tactic is used frequently, especially with younger children.

Once children are aware that what is happening to them is wrong, they often feel a sense of guilt over the abuse. They may also experience self-destructive thoughts or a loss of trust or self-esteem. Some of these signs may not even be obvious until the child becomes an adult. At first, he or she may deny that anything has happened when asked, or will not tell the whole story the first time.

It is estimated that between one in 4 children to one in 10 children will become a victim of sexual abuse before turning 18. "For many, it may be difficult to comprehend that a child would not immediately run to tell someone – mom, dad, a teacher, sibling, grandparent – after experiencing sexual abuse. Unfortunately, silence or delayed disclosure is actually the norm, rather than the exception". One estimate cites that 73 percent of children don't disclose sexual abuse for at least one year, 45 percent don't tell anyone for five years, and others never disclose their abuse at all.[16]

Thankfully, this door is no longer closed for me. I've opened it. I've forgiven the abusers. I share my story and will share it a thousand times again to expose this door and to let others know we do not have to be trapped behind it. This door did not destroy my life, nor is it the end of my story. And it doesn't have to destroy you or be the end of yours, either.

Just like a prisoner who has been released, we're free to share what was meant for evil in our lives. We can share with others how God brought us through this door and that He is willing to do the same for them. No more walking around in shame. God receives all the glory.

If you are having struggles or know of a child or someone who may be experiencing this type of door, I encourage you to seek assistance and reach out for help (see "Resources" at the end of this book). If you are a parent, please, please, *please* pay attention to your children and be open to listening to what they're saying. Do not only listen; take action. I've seen the tears and listened to story after story of those who've said:

"But I didn't know",

"He didn't tell me",

"I thought she was just acting out",

"I thought she just didn't want me to be with him", or

"I loved him. I didn't think he would do something like that."

No one knows what goes on behind closed doors. This door is one that has been in existence for ages. You may have experienced this as a child. I encourage you to get involved and find out more on this topic. You never know when you may be faced with this door. There are many resources available today. If you or your child is in immediate danger, you should always phone 911.

RANDY'S DOOR

Have you ever hated someone so much and said to yourself that you were finished with them or that you didn't want to have anything else to do with them? That's the way I felt about my mom. It started when I was around 8 years old. We were living with my grandparents.

My mom would leave on the weekend and at times stay gone for days. I cried in the mirror, saying to myself, "If she loved me, she would be here." Then she got arrested. I didn't understand. I was upset and angry at the world. I didn't know why it was happening.

She got out of jail and I thought that was it. But it wasn't. It started again. Not only that, she got pregnant. She had my brother. I thought she was fine after my brother was born. But she wasn't. I found what I thought was a cigarette in her purse. It wasn't and I felt betrayed. She told me she was done with it. I was disappointed, hurt, and angry at her. I tried to suppress my anger.

One night I was in the living room and saw a taxi pull up and my mom leave. I found my brother crying in the room. At that point, I was fed up. I hated her so much for what she was doing to my grandparents and us. This was a lot to handle as a kid. It was a constant battle of back and forth and being mad at her and everybody else for not doing anything.

Then it happened again. She got pregnant. I didn't really want her to keep the baby. This would be another mouth for my grandparents to feed. My mom was eventually sentenced to prison while she was pregnant. My baby brother was born while she was incarcerated. Although I was upset that she was pregnant and my grandparents would have another mouth to feed, I wouldn't trade him for the world.

I wrote a letter to my mom when she was in prison. The only reason I wrote it was to tell her how angry I was with her:

Amanda. I don't even know what to say to you. You do not understand how much pain I have to see in Ma-maw and Pa-paw. You don't understand how much pain I have. I had to tell Phillip that I don't know where his mommy and daddy are. The disappointment in his face and the sadness in his voice and eyes made me break down into tears. You have broken this family. You think that "I love you" and "I miss you" helps at all? I didn't get this job because I like waking up and busting my (expletive). I got it so I could provide for the children that you decided drugs and your friends were more important than. You cannot begin to imagine the hurt that you have left. I told you that it was going to catch up to you. I told you, and Ma-maw told you, that you would lose your son. I warned you so many (expletive) times. You just couldn't seem to get that through your head. How come it took you this long for you to attempt to show you give a (expletive)? All this time, and now you think I want to hear this? You use to be my world. You were who I wanted the most. I never wanted to believe the things people said. I didn't want to believe that my mother, the woman who I loved so much, was getting (expletive) instead of taking care of her child. I would call you at 2 in the morning crying, begging for you to come back. Do you remember that? I'm glad that my eyes were opened to the real Amanda because it turned me into a strong young man. The one good thing all this (expletive) has done for me. This has been too much. I am (expletive) done. I told you a long time ago that you'd lose me, and that's exactly what happened.

She was released from prison and came home again. I would avoid her as much as possible when she returned home. She found a job but had no transportation. My grandmother would have me drive her to work. I refused to talk to her on the ride. She would tell me that she loved me when she got out of the car and I had no response other than, "Bye". I still didn't want to have anything to do with her. I had accepted the fact that she was gone to me and I was through with her. I didn't want anything to do with her anymore.

A close friend who I opened up to knew how I felt about my mom. He told me I needed to hug my mom. He said it would be good for both of us. I felt she didn't deserve it. My friend wouldn't let up, convinced me, and I went to her job and hugged her. On the way home, I cried. I didn't know what to feel. I didn't know how to process it. I still didn't talk to her much. But then, I began to actually see some change in her. She was trying to make a difference. She was attending church and volunteering in the community. This was different.

I found forgiveness through God. I forgave my mom. The hate was moving out of my heart. My mom and I are in a really good place now. We talk almost every day. It's almost like nothing ever happened. I later wrote another letter to my mom:

I want to apologize to you. I have been selfish and it's because of pain brought to me through my life. You are an amazing mother with a beautiful soul and I am so sorry for not saying this sooner. I love you and I thank you for what you've done.

The card I gave you on Mother's Day was real. You've taught me how to be a person and showed me the path I need to take. I'm sorry for growing up too fast and I'm sorry for not being there. I'm sorry for turning my back on you. I'm so proud of you and what you have done.... God has moved through you and it's beautiful. ...I don't want you or anyone else in this house to think that I hate you. I'm figuring out life and I'm gaining wisdom from a lot of people. Life's amazing but it's unpredictable. I'm learning though. The other day I visited an elderly home and I talked to a group of people about life. It was eye-opening and they taught me a lot. I'm writing one of these for Ma-maw and Pa-paw as well so do not let them read this. Theirs will come soon enough. I love you, Randy.

It's hard to think that I held that much hate and anger for so long. I've grown a lot as a result of what I experienced. I've gotten better with forgiveness as a whole. I've learned to love people and not just turn away from them when they do me wrong. I've worked at accepting everybody for who they are instead of just casting them out.

DOORS OF COMPROMISE

Compromise. It's described a few different ways: giving up some demands and agreeing on a happy medium, reducing one's standards, or simply making concessions.

A compromise is rarely an act of accident or mistake. It is usually a deliberate course that seeks to find life on our terms. It's when we know what the truth is and we mix it with lesser issues, desires, or causes. Compromise can be tricky because it can offer what is genuinely good, but in exchange, it demands you give up what is best for you.

Joseph could have compromised, laid down his standards, and slept with Potiphar's wife. This lady did not let up and hounded him like a dog in heat to lay with her, but he refused. He considered laying with another man's wife adultery, which was a sin against God. Even when she caught him by his cloak, saying, "Come to bed with me!" Joseph left his cloak and ran out of the house (Genesis 39:7-12). Joseph's refusal put him at risk of being treated hostile by Potiphar's wife. Some would have called Joseph a punk for not seizing the opportunity. However, Joseph is an example of a God-fearing man of conviction. He proved to be honorable and uncompromising.

Compromise, for those following the Lord, often begins with leaving their first love, Jesus. This leads to the road of sin. If there is a breakdown in your relationship with God, it is only a matter of time until compromises start making their way into your life and you start lowering your standards here and there. Compromise happens when we see no value or importance in what God says.

The Bible warns us of many pitfalls that either tempt us or reveal compromise.

For everything in the world — the lust of the flesh, the lust of the eyes, and the pride of life — comes not from the Father but from the world. The world and its desires pass away, but whoever does the will of God lives forever.
-1 John 2:16-17

Second Timothy 4:3-4 says:

For the time will come when people will not put up with sound doctrine. Instead, to suit their own desires, they will gather around them a great number of teachers to say what their itching ears want to hear. They will turn their ears away from the truth and turn aside to myths.

COMPROMISE VS TRUTH

Let's be honest. Most people want to hear what they want to hear and have what they want to have. The uncorrupted truth seems to be a thing of the past. We want our cake and icing served just like we want to suit our fancy. If we can't get it here, we go over there. If this church doesn't preach the way we see or it doesn't align with our lifestyle, then we find another one or start our own. You know, like the Burger King slogan: "Have It Your Way".

Everyone tends to have their truth or their opinion. This is nothing new. We see it in Judges 21:25 when every man did what was right in his own eyes. They acted without God and came up with their own solutions. Does this describe the times we're living in now? This one thing is for sure: "A person may think their own ways are right, but the LORD weighs the heart" (Proverbs 21:2). Each of us will give an account of ourselves to God (Romans 14:12).

God has given us His Truth and his opinion on all matters. The truth is found in His Word, which is forever settled. No power – to include the government, our friends, Facebook, or national news – can change it. If we're committed to following Him, then His truth should be *our* truth. His truth is what we should speak, not our opinion. Jesus is the way, the truth, and the life. So, let's keep following Him.

Have you noticed the number of people who fail to stand for the truth because they don't want to hurt others' feelings? News Flash: They don't mind hurting yours. We should always stand up for His truth and stand by what is right (in His eyes). If not, we will continue to live like a pagan world heading towards hell in a handbasket, becoming completely ruined. Paul talked about this in Romans:

They exchanged the truth about God for a lie, and worshiped and served created things rather than the Creator — who is forever praised. Amen.
-Romans 1:25

NO VALUE OR IMPORTANCE

Most people tend to give attention to the things they value. If you don't believe me, ask some football fans how their team ranked during the season. But then there are times we don't appreciate the value of something or someone until it is taken away from us. We've observed this in our lives and that of others. Value is described as the regard that something is held to deserve, the importance, worth, or usefulness of something.

Often, we take for granted our next breath, our health, our parents, our children, our marriage, our friends, our jobs, our freedom, and the list goes on. But when they're not there, we say, "If only I had..." Would've, should've, and could've are too late.

You only have to look around and see where value is placed. Even the sanctity of life continues to decline. There are shootings and killings every day. Look at the decline in the values of family. Marriage used to be pure and unconditional. Children are being left to raise themselves while parents are out doing their thing, and the cycle continues. We try to place blame on the government, the "system," or others, and fail to examine ourselves. And we wonder why the world and our lives are in their current state. We've compromised and forgotten the values of love, respect, and responsibility.

We live our lives and say to ourselves, *Oh, it's nothing, it's not going to hurt,* or *that's just the way it is.* It is these things that seem so meaningless that grow into what we did not want or expect. It only takes one compromising word to spark a riot. We've seen this happen time and time again. How many lives and families will have to be destroyed? At what point will we see the importance of standing for the truth and stop compromising? Will it be when we have lost loved ones? Will it be when we no longer have good health? Or, is it maybe when we find ourselves behind prison bars?

Somehow, we manage to experience times in our lives where we have distanced ourselves from God and have chosen to operate like everyone else. We tend to see no value in loving the Lord, our God, with all our heart and with all our soul, and loving our neighbors as ourselves. Jesus would not have told us to do this if it wasn't important. He wants us to have life and that more abundantly (John 10:10). This doesn't happen on our terms, but His terms.

Compromise has worked its way like yeast through a batch of dough. Just like the yeast affects the dough, our choices affect others and their decisions. We should value those things that really matter. Do you value God? Is He important to you? Jonathan McReynolds sings in the song, "Make Room":

I find space for what I treasure
I make time for what I want
I choose my priorities and
Jesus you're my number one

Have you made room for Him? Is He your Number One? Take the time and reflect on what you are giving attention to and what you value. History is full of those who either did or did not see the value or importance of God. We dare not point fingers too quickly because we're no exception. We've been guilty as well. But we don't have to continue in that state. We can repent and start the change right now.

Paul wrote to the Romans that ignoring God leads to a downward spiral. Romans 1:28-32 (MSG) says:

Since they didn't bother to acknowledge God, God quit bothering them and let them run loose. And then all hell broke loose: rampant evil, grabbing and grasping, vicious backstabbing. They made life hell on earth with their envy, wanton killing, bickering, and cheating. Look at them: mean-spirited, venomous, fork-tongued God-bashers. Bullies, swaggerers, insufferable windbags! They keep inventing new ways of wrecking lives. They ditch their parents when they get in the way. Stupid, slimy, cruel, cold-blooded. And it's not as if they don't know better. They know perfectly well they're spitting in God's face. And they don't care – worse, they hand out prizes to those who do the worst things best!

Do you see that the Romans followed their desires and compromised? The scary part is that God quit bothering them and let them run loose. Do you see any resemblance to our world? Does this make you wonder if God has quit bothering us and turned us loose? Something to think about, isn't it?

You will notice in 1 Kings 16 that Ahab's kingdom was compromising by sinning with worthless idols. Ahab did more evil in the eyes of the Lord than any of the kings before him. He saw no value or importance in following God's instructions. And then he married Jezebel. She persuaded him to introduce the worship of the Tyrian god Baal-Melkart, a nature god. She tried to destroy those who opposed her; most of the prophets of God were killed at her command (1 Kings 18:4). Here's a side note: leave the Jezebels alone and be careful who you marry.

In 1 Kings 18, God sent Elijah with a message for Ahab. And then there was a meeting of the people on Mount Carmel, to include the 450 prophets of Baal and the 400 prophets of Asherah, who ate at Jezebel's table. Elijah said to them, "How long will you waver between two opinions? If the LORD is God, follow him; but if Baal is God, follow him" (1 Kings 18:21).

Elijah's question is still relevant today. How long will we waver between two opinions? This is like being double-minded. James says a double-minded man is unstable in all he does (James 1:8). Have you ever observed a person who can't make up his or her mind? We called these types of people "wishy-washy" in my day.

Take a look at the House of God. It has become difficult to tell the difference between the world and God's church. We see churches splitting over things that are plainly written in the Word. The Word is supposed to be the Church's rulebook. How did the church go from teaching the uncompromising Word of God to wanting to be popular with the world? Romans 12:2 tells us not to conform to the pattern of this world, but be transformed by the renewing of our mind. God's church is called to be the salt of the earth and the light of the world (Matthew 5:13-16). We've integrated the world into the church and made concessions in attempts to be politically correct and to show love (at least that's what we say). We're becoming a church filled with a bunch of compromisers. God set the standard. We can call it (whatever "it" may be) what we want, but it doesn't change the truth He established.

"A lie doesn't become truth
Wrong doesn't become right
And evil doesn't become good
Just because it's accepted by a majority."
-Booker T. Washington

We don't have to go along to get along. So, what if the majority doesn't agree with you or you with them? Doing right may inspire or convict someone. Oh! By the way, you can expect the dislikes, too. You're not alone. Read the scriptures and you will see that Jesus didn't agree with the majority, nor did the majority agree with Him. And He had plenty of dislikes. Let's stop calling right, wrong and wrong, right to try to suit our fancy or fit in. We don't have to be deceived. The devil played that trick on Eve. Look at their conversation in Genesis 3:1-6:

"...Did God really say, 'You must not eat from any tree in the garden'?"

The woman said to the serpent, "We may eat fruit from the trees in the garden, but God did say, 'You must not eat fruit from the tree that is in the middle of the garden, and you must not touch it, or you will die.'"

"You will not certainly die," the serpent said to the woman. "For God knows that when you eat from it your eyes will be opened, and you will be like God, knowing good and evil."

When the woman saw that the fruit of the tree was good for food and pleasing to the eye, and also desirable for gaining wisdom, she took some and ate it. She also gave some to her husband, who was with her, and he ate it.

Stay away from the forbidden fruit. Don't eat the compromise.

The Truth (the Word of God) is and will always be the Truth. It doesn't matter if we have a new fad, times change, or we see things differently. It is forever settled, and no law, political party, or you or I can change it. You see:

Heaven and earth will pass away, but my words will never pass away.
-Matthew 24:35

Your word, LORD, is eternal; it stands firm in the heavens.
-Psalm 119:89

Our opinions tend to change like the weather. They're either sunny, rainy, snowy, cloudy, partly cloudy, or windy. If we haven't figured it out, it's not our opinions that matter, but His. Say and do what He says and let's stop compromising.

LEARN FROM HISTORY

As we look and learn from history, we'll see that compromising never worked for the good. Let's examine some key examples of compromise from some of the Old Testament's most prominent lives: King Solomon, Samson, and the Israelites.

King Solomon:
He's David's son. Yes, David, the one who God said was "a man after his own heart" (1 Samuel 13:14). While on his death bed, David left these words to Solomon:

"I am about to go the way of all the earth," he said. "So be strong, act like a man, and observe what the LORD your God requires: Walk in obedience to him, and keep his decrees and commands, his laws and regulations, as written in the Law of Moses. Do this so that you may prosper in all you do and wherever you go and that the LORD may keep his promise to me: 'If your descendants watch how they live, and if they walk faithfully before me with all their heart and soul, you will never fail to have a successor on the throne of Israel.'
-1 Kings 2:2-4

Now, let's take a glimpse and see how this played out in the life of Solomon. He asked for a discerning heart to govern God's people and to distinguish between right and wrong. God was pleased and said:

..."Since you have asked for this and not for long life or wealth for yourself, nor have asked for the death of your enemies but for discernment in administering justice, I will do what you have asked. I will give you a wise and discerning heart, so that there will never have been anyone like you, nor will there ever be. Moreover, I will give you what you have not asked for – both wealth and honor – so that in your lifetime you will have no equal among kings. And if you walk in obedience to me and keep my decrees and commands as David your father did, I will give you a long life."
-1 Kings 3:7-14

What an awesome request – a discerning heart and to distinguish between right and wrong. Look at the last sentence of God's response, "And if you walk in obedience to me and keep my decrees and commands as David your father did, I will give you a long life." What a promise! However, at some point,

Solomon became relaxed and compromised. Read 1 Kings 11:1-13. He loved many foreign women besides Pharaoh's daughter. The foreign women were from the nations which the Lord had said, "You must not intermarry with them, because they will surely turn your hearts after their gods" (1 Kings 11:2). Solomon loved them – all 700 wives and 300 concubines. And they did just what the Lord said: led him astray and turned his heart after other gods. Solomon chose to disobey God's instructions and he was held accountable for his decision:

So the LORD said to Solomon, "Since this is your attitude and you have not kept my covenant and my decrees, which I commanded you, I will most certainly tear the kingdom away from you and give it to one of your subordinates. Nevertheless, for the sake of David your father, I will not do it during your lifetime. I will tear it out of the hand of your son. Yet I will not tear the whole kingdom from him, but will give him one tribe for the sake of David my servant and for the sake of Jerusalem, which I have chosen."
-1 Kings 11:11-13

Seven hundred wives and 300 hundred concubines. WOW! I'm still trying to picture this and figure out why Solomon needed so many. Do you get it? It only takes one to drive you crazy. (Oops, I'm a wife of 46 years. Hopefully, I'm not driving my Fred crazy.)

Solomon did not have to compromise. It appears he may have gotten the picture later. He said, "I amassed silver and gold for myself, and the treasure of kings and provinces. I acquired male and female singers, and a harem as well–the delights of a man's heart" (Ecclesiastes 2:8). Then he said, "...I denied myself nothing my eyes desired; I refused my heart no pleasure..." (Ecclesiastes 2:10). He said, "...everything was meaningless, a chasing after the wind; nothing was gained under the sun" (Ecclesiastes 2:11). He gives the conclusion in Ecclesiastes 12:13 (MSG): "...The last and final word is this: Fear God. Do what he tells you."

Solomon's words, "Fear God. Do what he tells you," are

indeed words of wisdom. Following God's word will keep us off the road of compromise.

Samson:

Samson is one of the judges who ruled over Israel before the time of the kings (Judges 13-16). He was dedicated from birth to God to be a Nazarite. He would also save the Israelites from the Philistines. Those who took the Nazarite vow were subject to some strict rules. Read Numbers 6:3-8.

Picture this. Samson has the power of Superman. He's a one-man act using his God-given strength. He is side-tracked and fools around, falling in love with a Philistine woman, Delilah. Now if that isn't some kind of a match – a Nazarite dedicated to God and a Philistine who doesn't serve God. I am just saying.

Unknowingly to Samson, Delilah was tasked to find the secret of his strength. Three times she begs to know the secret, and three times he lies to her. Delilah didn't give up. Just like the devil, isn't it? Samson finally tells her: "No razor has ever been used on my head because I have been a Nazarite dedicated to God from my mother's womb. If my head were shaved, my strength would leave me, and I would become as weak as any other man" (Judges 16:17).

Sure enough, Delilah got the information she wanted. If only Samson had been as persistent as Delilah. Instead, he continued to compromise, fell asleep, and woke up with a bald head. His hair had been shaved and God's power had left him. Delilah handed Samson over to the Philistines, who gouged out his eyes and forced him to grind at a mill in prison.

Samson chose to compromise. He failed to recognize or heed the danger signs. But that is how compromise works. We will encounter many Delilahs in this world who seek to find our weakness and exploit it. Don't give in. It's not worth it.

The Israelites:

The Israelites constantly turned their back on the Lord. Psalm 78:56-57 says, "But they put God to the test and rebelled against the Most High; they did not keep his statutes. Like their ancestors they were disloyal and faithless, as unreliable as a faulty bow."

In 1 Samuel 7 and 8, Samuel, a judge of Israel, told the people that God would deliver them out of the hand of the Philistines if they rid themselves of the foreign gods and committed themselves to the Lord and served Him only. They did and God delivered them. They later asked to have a king appointed, like all the other nations, to lead them. This displeased Samuel; so, he prayed to the Lord. Here is how the Lord replied:

And the LORD told him: "Listen to all that the people are saying to you; it is not you they have rejected, but they have rejected me as their king. As they have done from the day I brought them up out of Egypt until this day, forsaking me and serving other gods, so they are doing to you. Now listen to them; but warn them solemnly and let them know what the king who will reign over them will claim as his rights."
-1 Samuel 8:7-9

Read the rest of 1 Samuel 8 to see the warnings they were given of having a king. I would have stuck with the Lord. The Israelites refused to listen to Samuel and still insisted on having a king over them. They wanted to be like all the other nations with a king to lead them and to go out before them and fight their battles. Who did they think had fought their battles? They got more than they asked for and it wasn't good. They forgot their God, the King of all kings.

Do you see any similarities with history and where we are today? Did you notice that even in biblical times, God didn't tread lightly when it came to sin and compromise? And it's the same today. He, nor His standard, has changed.

IT'S NOT AN ITCH OR SCRATCH

We've observed the compromising of others and our own. We treat it like an itch or scratch. However, it is not a case of taking some medicine to treat the symptoms, or even placing a bandage to cover up the scratch.

Compromising can be as life-threatening as sepsis. Sepsis is the body's extreme response to an infection. It is a life-threatening medical emergency. Sepsis happens when an infection you already have, such as in your skin, lungs, urinary tract, or somewhere else, triggers a chain reaction throughout your body. Without timely treatment, sepsis can rapidly lead to tissue damage, organ failure, and death. Let's be aggressive to treat and stop compromising in its tracks.

The scriptures are clear about compromising when it comes to God's standards. Psalm 119:1-8 (MSG) says:

You're blessed when you stay on course, walking steadily on the road revealed by GOD. You're blessed when you follow his directions, doing your best to find him. That's right — you don't go off on your own; you walk straight along the road he set.
You, GOD, prescribed the right way to live; now you expect us to live it. Oh, that my steps might be steady, keeping to the course you set; Then I'd never have any regrets in comparing my life with your counsel. I thank you for speaking straight from your heart; I learn the pattern of your righteous ways. I'm going to do what you tell me to do; don't ever walk off and leave me.

This applies to all areas of our lives, including our relationships. Remember Samson and Solomon. How many times have you heard, "Do not be bound together with unbelievers?" Yet we see it happening often. A Christian falling in love with a non-Christian. Haven't you heard the excuses:

I'm going to lead them to the Lord? or
I've prayed about it and I have peace?

Stop kidding yourself. Leading them to the Lord, praying about it, and having peace in this instance are defined as excuses, disobedience, and compromise. And it doesn't matter how we try to explain it away or say God understands. What He understands is obedience, and if we love Him, we will keep His commands (John 14:15).

King Saul found out that compromising was not an itch or scratch. He lost his kingship for failure to follow God's command:

"You have done a foolish thing," Samuel said. "You have not kept the command the LORD your God gave you; if you had, he would have established your kingdom over Israel for all time. But now your kingdom will not endure; the LORD has sought out a man after his own heart and appointed him ruler of his people, because you have not kept the LORD's command."
-1 Samuel 13:13-14

WHEN WE REFUSE COMPROMISE

Life is all about choices, and we are the ones who get to choose. Just like forgiveness, the choice to compromise is all ours. No one can make you, not even the devil. So, no more excuses centering on how the devil "made" you do it. Look in the mirror and you will see a reflection. It's you. You made you do it. No more blaming God like Adam did when he said, "The woman you gave me," (Genesis 3:12) or Eve saying, "The serpent deceived me, and I ate" (Genesis 3:13). The choice is ours. Let's look at more examples in scripture of how people handled compromise.

Micaiah:
In 1 Kings 22, Ahab asked Jehoshaphat to go with him to fight against Ramoth Gilead. Jehoshaphat agreed but wanted to seek God's counsel first. Ahab brought together his prophets — about 400 hundred men — and asked them, "Shall I go to war against Ramoth Gilead, or shall I refrain?" They told him to go

and the Lord would give him victory. But Jehoshaphat still wanted to hear from a prophet of the Lord.

Ahab told him there was still one prophet, Micaiah, through whom they could inquire of the Lord, but that he hated him because he never prophesied anything good about him. A messenger went to get Micaiah and said to him, "Look, the other prophets without exception are predicting success for the king. Let your word agree with theirs, and speak favorably." Micaiah wasn't intimidated:

But Micaiah said, "As surely as the LORD lives, I can tell him only what the LORD tells me."
-1 King 22:14

Micaiah told Ahab, "...the Lord has put a deceiving spirit in the mouths of all these prophets of yours. The Lord has decreed disaster for you" (1 Kings 22:23). One of Ahab's men slapped Micaiah in the face and the king had Micaiah thrown into a dungeon and fed only bread and water. He was to remain in prison until Ahab's return. Still unintimidated, Micaiah said, "If you ever return safely, the LORD has not spoken through me." Then he added, "Mark my words, all you people! ..." Read 1 Kings 22 to see the rest of the story. Micaiah didn't compromise and said what God told him to say.

Peter and John:
In Acts 4, Peter and John were teaching the people and proclaiming in Jesus the resurrection of the dead. More than 5,000 men heard and believed their message. This disturbed the religious people. The priests, the captain of the temple guard, and the Sadducees seized them and they were put in jail. The rulers, elders, and the teachers of the law met with them and warned them not to speak or teach at all in the name of Jesus. Peter and John were not having it:

But Peter and John replied, "Which is right in God's eyes: to listen to you, or to him? You be the judges! As for us, we cannot help speaking about what we have seen and heard."
-Acts 4:19-20

Do these guys sound like they're intimidated? They could have compromised and hushed up. But they had no problem standing up for the truth. What about you? When is the last time you've told someone you were going to speak what you've seen and heard about Jesus?

Daniel, Shadrach, Meshack, and Abednego:

These young men were captives in a foreign land and chosen to serve in the king's court. They were to eat the royal food and drink wine provided by the king, but in honor of God's law, they resolved not to defile themselves. They chose not to compromise. In response to their decision, God caused the official to show favor and compassion to them. When it came to matters of wisdom and understanding about which the king questioned them, Daniel, Shadrach, Meshack and Abednego were found to be ten times better than all the magicians and enchanters in his whole kingdom that ate a daily amount of food and wine from the king's table (Daniel 1:5-20).

GET OFF THE FENCE

Let's look again at 1 Kings 18:21 in The Message version. Elijah challenged the people: "How long are you going to sit on the fence? If GOD is the real God, follow him; if it's Baal, follow him. Make up your minds!"

It's time to choose. How long are you going to sit on the fence? I can't imagine sitting on a fence. The ones I've seen don't strike me as being comfortable. They could tear and cause harm to some body parts. Matthew 6:24 is a picture of sitting on the fence and trying to serve two masters. It has to be either our way or God's way.

Stop sitting on the fence of compromise and make a choice. Have you ever been in a restaurant and the people at the other table took 30 minutes looking at the menu and still can't seem to decide what to order? Picture this going on while you're on your lunch break or on a schedule. Doesn't this make you want to place their order for them? I'm just saying. I'm still a work in progress because I get annoyed when someone won't commit and won't make and stick to a decision. Pick a side. If the outcome isn't what you thought it would be, then you know better the next time. That's how we learn.

Joshua didn't sit on the fence. He said:

"Now fear the Lord and serve him with all faithfulness. ...But if serving the LORD seems undesirable to you, then choose for yourselves this day whom you will serve, whether the gods your ancestors served beyond the Euphrates, or the gods of the Amorites, in whose land you are living. But as for me and my household, we will serve the LORD."
-Joshua 24:14-15

Pause Break - Pause Break!

Are you still on the fence? If so, why? Life isn't stopping because you're sitting there. There will come a time when you're tired of sitting there and wonder why your life is still in its state. But you don't have to wait until then. Get off, now. What do you have to lose? Not a thing. Now choose sides - the "not to compromise" side.

In Matthew 25:1-13, Jesus tells a story about a party of ten virgins chosen to participate in a wedding. Each of them is carrying a lamp or torch as they await the coming of the bridegroom, which they expect at some time during the night. Five of the virgins are wise and have brought oil for their lamps. Five are foolish and have only brought their lamps. At midnight, all the virgins hear the call to come out to meet the bridegroom. Realizing their lamps have gone out, the foolish virgins ask the wise ones for oil, but they refuse, saying that there will certainly not be enough for them to share. While the foolish virgins are away trying to get more oil, the bridegroom arrives. The wise virgins then accompany him to the celebration. The others arrive too late.

".. 'Lord, Lord,' they said, 'open the door for us!'

"But he replied, 'Truly I tell you, I don't know you.'

"Therefore keep watch, because you do not know the day or the hour."

I wonder if the five foolish virgins wished they had thought about their decision. By the time they probably did, it was too late. Are you being wise in your choices or are you compromising, thinking you have time to get it together or be ready?

Let me ask you this. Are you prepared to meet Jesus or have you been sitting on the fence? Choose a side, like Joshua did in Joshua 24:15, and serve the Lord. And if you have already chosen His side, don't play with compromising.

Compromising isn't hiding under a bushel or tree. Jesus gave a warning, "There is nothing concealed that will not be disclosed, or hidden that will not be made known" (Luke 12:2).

Think about this. What if it is as Jesus said in Luke 12:20, "...This very night your life will be demanded from you," in the parable of the rich fool? Would compromising be worth it then? Is compromising worth being excluded from being with the Lord forevermore?

Something else to think about: are you on the fence of compromise? Do you try to play it safe and stay in the middle? Are you resembling the world so much that you look and act like the people in it rather than acting like Jesus? If you were on trial for doing the right thing, would you be found guilty as charged? What does your life display? Where do you stand on the command listed in the following table? Write your response in the table.

The Word Says...	Your Response...
..."Love the Lord your God with all your heart and with all your soul and with all your mind. This is the first and greatest commandment. And the second is like it: 'Love your neighbor as yourself.'" Matthew 22:37-39	

If only we could understand the importance of not compromising the way that people flocked to the gas stations when they learned of a hack and the possibility of a gas shortage in May 2021. Yes, having gasoline for our vehicles is important. But compromising truth is a matter of life or death.

Don't be fooled: we will all be placed in compromising positions at one point or another. If you haven't, keep on living. If left unchecked, compromise will lead to sin. So don't deceive yourself (1 John 1:8).

Now, there is a difference between the person who is sorry and repents for sin and the one who continually sins over and over again and doesn't repent and thinks, "It's okay. God will forgive me. God will give me grace." That's not how it works. Read Romans 6:1.

I ask you again, is the door of compromise worth being excluded? Then, stop it. Join me and let's repent, re-dedicate, or make a commitment to no longer compromise. Let's stand for truth, obey, and follow the Lord.

Here are more doors that others have experienced.

ROBERT'S DOOR

I had several girlfriends and played around. I never thought about marriage. But then I met Jen. It was love at first sight. She caught my heart. We dated two years and later married. We were inseparable. We were the picture of a perfect couple. We later had a son and daughter.

I started a new job. I was the new guy in the shop. The other guys would get together after work and on the weekends. They invited me to join them. I didn't go at first. I thought about it later. What could it hurt? I saw it as an opportunity to bond and fit in with the guys.

It turned out to be more. Guys weren't the only ones getting together. While with them, I began to do some things that were not in keeping with who I was and my marriage vows. I made a mistake. Well, the truth is it wasn't a mistake. I knew it was wrong. I compromised right for wrong to fit in with them. I'm not blaming the guys. They didn't make me do what I did. I made the choice. You feel like your manhood is questioned when you don't go along. I hadn't planned for things to turn out as they did.

I walked around feeling guilty and afraid my wife would find out. No one told her, but she noticed a difference and confronted me. I don't know if that was a woman's intuition or guilt written all over my face. I hurt my wife and she could no longer trust me. I lost my marriage and family behind compromising. Trying to fit in and be like the guys wasn't worth it. Don't do it.

MICHELLE'S DOOR

It seems that my life has been full of compromise. Where do I start? I wanted to fit in. So, when you want to fit in, you do what others are doing. You can't be different.

I became pregnant at age 16 while trying to fit in. The father of my child was my first love and first intimate partner. He was everything to me. He left me after I became pregnant. He wouldn't even acknowledge our child as his. Needless to say, this broke my heart. I felt like I had been used.

Here I was a teenager about to have a child. What did I know about raising a baby? I was still being raised. I'm thankful that I had family that stood by my side, especially my mother. I wouldn't have made it without her.

My life was set and I knew what I was going to do. Before I had gotten pregnant, my goal was to finish high school and go to college. Everything was in place to accomplish that, but a baby wasn't part of it. So, those plans to go to college were shattered. I was embarrassed and at times felt worthless. That's the cost of compromise.

My baby (a boy) was born healthy. He knew who his daddy was even if he had not seen him since he was 5 years old. Emotionally, I was a mess. I didn't know why. My body was changing. I kept a lot of things inside. I experienced mood swings and anxiety. I was depressed.

I did not realize until years later how this affected me. To be honest, it affected all areas of my life. You don't know how your past affects your present. I had blocked so many things out that happened during that time.

It would be more than 15 years later that the father of my son and I would be in the same room. I had always wondered why he treated me as he did. He knew the truth about our son and abandoned us. Without even thinking about it, I asked the question. I asked him "why". I had always thought the problem was me. This conversation unleashed something within me that I didn't realize I had been carrying. As we talked, I felt a weight being lifted off me.

The road I had to travel could have been avoided if I hadn't tried to fit in and trust that the people I tried to fit in with were trustworthy. If I knew what I know now, I would like to think that I wouldn't have tried to fit in. Compromising isn't worth it.

My son and I made it. I'm thankful I wasn't alone, and I can encourage you not to compromise. If you are compromising in any area of your life, I recommend you learn from my experience and the years that it took to regain my peace of mind. Stop and count the cost. Compromise is not worth it.

CLOSED DOORS

Everyone does not view closed doors the same. How do you view a closed door? Do you see it as being locked or having no access? What about being a dead end or a feeling that there's no way out? Is it a symbol of opportunity or protection to you?

Just as there are differences in views, we have several choices to make when we face a closed door. What action will we take? Do we push past being uncomfortable about not knowing what lies beyond the door? Will we turn back defeated by the barrier, or will we attempt to gain access? Will we trust the Lord? Will we remember that a closed door doesn't mean there is no access or that it is locked?

Joseph being sold into slavery appears to be a closed door. What would be the chances of a slave being freed? I would imagine he had no idea what door he would have to confront. However, this was not a closed door. This would be the road leading to the fulfillment of his dream. When I think of closed doors, I am reminded of my sister, Delores. She is 68 years old and has never walked a day in her life. She has outlived the life expectancy she was given by the doctors. She suffers from cerebral palsy among other things. She is my older sister although I tell her I feel I'm the oldest. Delores depends on others to assist in her care due to the disability. I have never heard her complain about not being able to walk, not even to God. She's always made the best of her situation.

As you can probably imagine, Delores has been confronted with many doors that appear to be closed. However, that has never been how she sees them. Just about the time we've given up or think she's given up on something, here she comes again. The doors that appear to be closed always open for her.

There was a time she wanted to compete in The Miss Wheelchair Alabama contest. There were many reasons she could not compete. The main one was she didn't have transportation (a wheelchair-accessible van) to get to Auburn, which was about two hours from Dothan. We had closed the door. But not Delores. Without our knowledge, she was still working on it. About two weeks later, she said, "I have a way to go". She arranged her transportation, with the help of Vaughn Blumberg Center, and competed in the contest. We were so proud of her.

There was another time when one of her case managers told her that it wasn't time for her to get a new wheelchair. Delores insisted that it was time and did not allow what was said to deter her. Needless to say, she was right and got her wheelchair. On another occasion, one of my sister's caregivers found a knot on Delores' breast. It was another door that she would have to face: cancer. I had to tell her this news. She made her choices about her treatment and handled this chapter in her life with such grace and confidence.

What amazes me about my sister is that she does not see her disability as a closed door. She's never attended school (although I remind her that we played school at home with her). She has a memory out of this world. We go to her when we've forgotten things from our childhood or things that occurred as recently as last week. She has a way of matching her clothes that would make a fashion designer wonder where she got her skills. We're always asking her where she's going all dolled up. One last thing that she has going for her is that besides our brother, Phillip, she is the apple of our mother's eye. I'm not kidding. My other sister, Janice, will tell you it's the truth.

Watching my sister encourages me to keep moving forward regardless of the doors I encounter. Her strength helps me eliminate any thought about closed doors that doesn't line up with God's word. Now, what's your excuse?

Do you have a disability? If so, do you see it as a closed door? If your answer is yes, then follow my sister's lead and keep charging. If you're still not convinced, maybe you need to talk to my sister.

Many may view their doors as closed for various reasons. Some doors may represent inadequacy, rejection, exclusion, protection, fear, or not trusting the Lord. Let's look at some closed doors, in scripture, in screenplay style.

JEREMIAH'S DOOR

God called Jeremiah to prophesy to proclaim Jerusalem's coming destruction by invaders from the north. This was because Israel had forsaken God by worshiping idols and burning their children as offerings to Baal. Jeremiah resisted the call by complaining that he was only a child and did not know how to speak. Now, let's go to the movies. Imagine this (my imaginary Oscar-winning) screenplay with Jeremiah and God:

ACTION – PLAY

God: "Before I formed you in the womb I knew you, before you were born I set you apart; I appointed you as a prophet to the nations."

Jeremiah: … "I do not know how to speak; I am too young."

God: "Do not say, 'I am too young.' You must go to everyone I send you to and say whatever I command you. Do not be afraid of them, for I am with you and will rescue you."

The LORD reaches out his hand and touches Jeremiah's mouth.

God: "I have put my words in your mouth. See, today I appoint you over nations and kingdoms to uproot and tear down, to destroy and overthrow, to build and to plant."

The Lord continues to speak to Jeremiah about how He has prepared him. He then tells Jeremiah what to do.

God: "Get yourself ready! Stand up and say to them whatever I command you. Do not be terrified by them, or I will terrify you before them. Today I have made you a fortified city, an iron pillar and a bronze wall to stand against the whole land — against the kings of Judah, its officials, its priests and the people of the land. They will fight against you but will not overcome you, for I am with you and will rescue you."

The full version of this screenplay may be found in Jeremiah 1. Go check it out.

We see Jeremiah at what he perceives as a closed door: his inadequacy of being a youth and his inability to speak. Do you think God knew this already? Well, He did, and paid no attention to Jeremiah's excuses. God reassured Jeremiah that He was going with him, that Jeremiah would speak His words, that he didn't have to fear the enemy, and that He would rescue Jeremiah when they fought against him. Jeremiah opened the closed door, went through it, and prophesied the Word of the Lord. And God did as He said.

Are you like Jeremiah? Has God called you to a task and you've viewed the door as closed? Have you thought about your inabilities and given excuses, too? Well, face the door and stop making excuses. The same God that was with Jeremiah will be with you. Just do what He tells you. It's not a closed door.

Let's keep rolling to the next screenplay.

MOSES' DOOR

Most of us have heard of Moses. What is one of your memories of him? My first memory is an old man – with a white beard and stick in his hand – standing on top of a mountain and pointing toward the sea. The waters were divided in the middle so the people could get to the other side. Well, that's the way it looked to me as Charlton Heston portrayed him in *The Ten Commandments* (a 1956 film). Do you remember that?

You can find Moses at a closed door in Exodus 3 and 4. God told Moses He was sending him to Pharaoh to bring His people, the Israelites, out of Egypt. Moses asks God, "Who am I that I should go to Pharaoh and bring the Israelites out of Egypt?" (Exodus 3:11). Can you relate to Moses?

ACTION - PLAY

God: "I will be with you. And this will be the sign to you that it is I who have sent you: When you have brought the people out of Egypt, you will worship God on this mountain."

Moses: "Suppose I go to the Israelites and say to them, 'The God of your fathers has sent me to you,' and they ask me, 'What is his name?' Then what shall I tell them?"

God: "I am who I am. This is what you are to say to the Israelites: 'I am has sent me to you.'"

Can you still relate to Moses? Moses had another question.

Moses: "What if they do not believe me or listen to me and say, 'The LORD did not appear to you'?"

God: "What is that in your hand?"

Moses: "A staff."

God: "Throw it on the ground."

Moses throws it on the ground and it becomes a snake. Moses runs. (And I would have, too.)

God: "Reach out your hand and take it by the tail."

Moses reaches out and takes hold of the snake and it turns back into a staff in his hand.

God: "This is so that they may believe that the LORD, the God of their fathers — the God of Abraham, the God of Isaac and the God of Jacob — has appeared to you."

God: "Put your hand inside your cloak."

Moses puts his hand into his cloak, and when he takes it out, the skin is leprous, white as snow.

God: "Now put it back into your cloak."

Moses puts his hand back into his cloak, and when he takes it out, it is restored, like the rest of his flesh.

What would you have done if you were Moses at this point? Moses still had something to say.

Moses: "Pardon your servant, Lord. I have never been eloquent, neither in the past nor since you have spoken to your servant. I am slow of speech and tongue."

God: "Who gave human beings their mouths? Who makes them deaf or mute? Who gives them sight or makes them blind? Is it not I, the LORD? Now go; I will help you speak and will teach you what to say."

Moses: "Pardon your servant, Lord. Please send someone else."

Moses has now angered God. God allowed him to use his brother, Aaron, as a mouthpiece since he could speak well. God speaks to Moses again.

God: "You shall speak to him and put words in his mouth; I will help both of you speak and will teach you what to do. He will speak to the people for you, and it will be as if he were your mouth and as if you were God to him. But take this staff in your hand so you can perform the signs with it."

The Lord told Pharaoh to let His people go. He refused. Then the LORD said to Moses, "Now you will see what I will do to Pharaoh: Because of my mighty hand he will let them go; because of my mighty hand he will drive them out of his country"(Exodus 6:1). It would take several plague demonstrations before Pharaoh got the picture and let them go (Exodus 12:31-32).

Pharaoh still had a problem after letting the Israelites leave. In Exodus 14, we see Pharaoh and his army pursuing the children of Israel. They overtook the Israelites camping by the sea beside Pi Hahiroth. Imagine the Israelites by the sea with a closed door in front of them and Pharaoh and his army behind them. Which way could they go? The children of Israel were afraid and cried out to the Lord. Moses said to the people:

..."Do not be afraid. Stand firm and you will see the deliverance the LORD will bring you today. The Egyptians you see today you will never see again. The LORD will fight for you; you need only to be still."
-Exodus 14:13-14

The Lord said to Moses:

"...Why are you crying out to me? Tell the Israelites to move on. Raise your staff and stretch out your hand over the sea to divide the water so that the Israelites can go through the sea on dry ground."
-Exodus 14:15-16

Moses and the people did as God said. The Israelites went through the sea on dry ground with a wall of water on their right and left.

That day the LORD saved Israel from the hands of the Egyptians, and Israel saw the Egyptians lying dead on the shore. And when the Israelites saw the mighty hand of the LORD displayed against the Egyptians, the people feared the LORD and put their trust in him and in Moses his servant.
-Exodus 14:30-31

There is so much more to Moses' story. Go research and finish the rest of the action-packed scenes. Moses had his excuses, and they appeared as closed doors. But God!

Let's see one more screenplay.

GIDEON'S DOOR

We read in Judges 6 that the Israelites did evil in the eyes of the Lord, and for seven years he gave them into the hands of the Midianites. They were afraid of the Midianites and would hide out in the mountains in caves and forts. Then there came a day that they cried out to the Lord for help.

Gideon, a judge over Israel, was hiding from the enemies on a threshing floor.   The angel of the Lord appeared to him.

ACTION - PLAY
Angel of the Lord: "The LORD is with you, mighty warrior."

Gideon: "Pardon me, my lord, but if the LORD is with us, why has all this happened to us? ... now the LORD has abandoned us and given us into the hand of Midian."

The Lord: "Go in the strength you have and save Israel out of Midian's hand. Am I not sending you?"

Gideon: "Pardon me, my lord, but how can I save Israel? My clan is the weakest in Manasseh, and I am the least in my family."

The Lord: "I will be with you, and you will strike down all the Midianites, leaving none alive."

Gideon: "If now I have found favor in your eyes, give me a sign that it is really you talking to me. Please do not go away until I come back and bring my offering and set it before you."

The Lord: "I will wait until you return."

Gideon prepares and brings his offering. Gideon realizes that it is the angel of the Lord.

Gideon: "Alas, Sovereign LORD! I have seen the angel of the LORD face to face!"

The Lord: "Peace! Do not be afraid. You are not going to die."

Gideon: "If you will save Israel by my hand as you have promised — look, I will place a wool fleece on the threshing floor. If there is dew only on the fleece and all the ground is dry, then I will know that you will save Israel by my hand, as you said."

Gideon rises early the next day; he squeezes the fleece and wrings out the dew — a bowl full of water.

Gideon: "Do not be angry with me. Let me make just one more request. Allow me one more test with the fleece, but this time make the fleece dry and let the ground be covered with dew."
The fleece is dry; all the ground is covered with dew. Gideon and all his men camp at the spring of Harod.

The Lord: "You have too many men. I cannot deliver Midian into their hands, or Israel would boast against me, 'My own strength has saved me.' Now announce to the army, 'Anyone who trembles with fear may turn back and leave Mount Gilead.'"

Twenty-two thousand men leave, while 10,000 remain.

The Lord: "There are still too many men. Take them down to the water, and I will thin them out for you there. If I say, 'This one shall go with you,' he shall go; but if I say, 'This one shall not go with you,' he shall not go."

Gideon takes the men down to the water.

The Lord: "Separate those who lap the water with their tongues as a dog laps from those who kneel down to drink."

Three hundred of them drink from cupped hands, lapping like dogs. All the rest get down on their knees to drink.

The Lord: "With the three hundred men that lapped I will save you and give the Midianites into your hands. Let all the others go home."

Gideon sent the rest of the Israelites home but kept the 300, who took over the provisions and trumpets of the others. They didn't even have to invade or attack to wipe out the Midianites. The 300 trumpets sounded and the Lord caused the men throughout the enemy camp to turn on each other with their swords.

Now, let's do the math:

- Gideon starts with 32,000.
- A total of 22,000 leave after the first cut, so he is left with 10,000.
- Then, 9,700 men leave.
- He is now left with 300.

It appeared the odds were stacked against him. It looked like a closed door. But God! A closed door? I say not. There is more to Gideons' story. Go check it out in Judges 6-7.

Pause Break – Pause Break!

There are times we can't see the big picture. We only see what is before us – the appearance of a closed door. We see our inadequacies or our fears. Have you been at this door before? What excuses have you made? Know this: If God calls us to it, He will not only provide what it takes but will bring us through it. Let's stop with the closed doors of excuses and do what God is calling us to do.

We read in Revelation 3:7-8:

…These are the words of him who is holy and true, who holds the key of David. What he opens no one can shut, and what he shuts no one can open. I know your deeds. See, I have placed before you an open door that no one can shut. I know that you have little strength, yet you have kept my word and have not denied my name.

The Message version says, "…I've opened a door before you that no one can slam shut." What a promise. No devil, no entity, no person – not a thing – can shut it. That is the God we serve.

If Balaam was still living today, I think he would tell you about his experience with God. Balaam was a seer, someone who followed the Lord and had a gift of visions, as well as the ability to speak blessings and curses. He would likely tell you, "You can't bless what God hasn't blessed or curse what God hasn't cursed." Balak, the King of Moab, was afraid of the Israelites because they had defeated everyone they encountered in battle. So, he called for Balaam to come and curse the Israelites in order to defeat them. In other words, he was trying to close a door that God had not closed.

"Now come and put a curse on these people, because they are too powerful for me. Perhaps then I will be able to defeat them and drive

them out of the land. For I know that whoever you bless is blessed, and whoever you curse is cursed."
-Numbers 22:6

God said to Balaam, "...Do not go with them. You must not put a curse on those people, because they are blessed" (Numbers 22:12).

As a result of God's command, Balaam refused to go. The king's messengers came again, and this time the Lord allowed Balaam to go, but he was only to do what the Lord told him (Numbers 22:20). Balaam spoke what the Lord said. As a matter of fact, he blessed the Israelites from all three locations that Balak repositioned him in hopes of getting a curse upon the Israelites. No matter how hard Balak tried, he couldn't touch God's people (Numbers 23-24).

IT'S NOT ALWAYS WHAT YOU THINK

You can't see beyond the closed door. Whatever is on the other side is out of sight. It's understandable that you may be somewhat reluctant. But you have to make a choice and take action to see what's there.

Think about this: a closed door does not always mean a locked door. God may be putting a hedge of protection around you. A closed door may simply be a redirection or opportunity to move on. A closed door may also mean that you may have taken your eyes off God.

Look at Joseph's story again. Doesn't it look like God had a hedge of protection around him? He was able to move on in spite of the appearance of closed doors. The doors may have appeared to be closed but they were never locked because God was with Joseph and always gave him favor.

Have you ever experienced a door that you thought was locked? I did. I recall a time when I wanted to get a government job. I heard that it would be hard to get one because it was very competitive, and even more so if you had never worked for the government before. A temporary clerical position was opened and advertised. I didn't want a temporary position but my husband, Fred, convinced me to apply. He said it would allow me to get my foot in the door. I applied and was scheduled for an interview. I drove around the post looking for the place and couldn't find it. Needless to say, I didn't get my foot in that door. But I didn't give up. Another position – this time a permanent one – was announced 30 days later. Fred didn't have to tell me to apply. I talked to the Lord about this position. My exact words were, "Lord, I didn't talk to you about that last job, but I want this job." I applied for the position. An interview was scheduled and I knew where to go this time. I interviewed, got my foot in the door, and got the job. I would later find out that I competed against 13 others who already had their feet in the door. This door led to other opened doors. I retired after 31 years of government service. God did it!

God may have closed a door temporarily, but it doesn't mean that it will be closed forever. Maybe it's not the right time. What if He has something else in mind for you? Or what if He wants to protect you? It's during these times that we have to trust Him and wait on His leading.

There are many instances of doors in the Bible that appear closed but weren't. Let's look at some of them.

Jailbreak (King Herod arrested Peter):
After arresting him, he put him in prison, handing him over to be guarded by four squads of four soldiers each. Herod intended to bring him out for public trial after the Passover. So Peter was kept in prison, but the church was earnestly praying to God for him. The night before Herod was to bring him to trial, Peter was sleeping between two soldiers, bound with two chains, and sentries stood guard at the entrance. Suddenly an angel of the Lord appeared and a light shone in the cell. He struck Peter on the side and woke him up. "Quick, get up!" he said, and the chains fell off Peter's wrists. Then the angel said to him, "Put on your clothes and sandals." And Peter did so. "Wrap your cloak around you and follow me," the angel told him. Peter followed him out of the prison, but he had no idea that what the angel was doing was really happening; he thought he was seeing a vision.

They passed the first and second guards and came to the iron gate leading to the city. It opened for them by itself, and they went through it. When they had walked the length of one street, suddenly the angel left him.
-Acts 12:4-10

Now, I am not advocating breaking out of jail. This was divine intervention, the angel of the Lord.

Man Paralyzed and Bedridden for Eight Years:
As Peter traveled about the country, he went to visit the Lord's people who lived in Lydda. There he found a man named Aeneas, who was paralyzed and had been bedridden for eight years. "Aeneas," Peter said to him, "Jesus Christ heals you. Get up and roll up your mat." Immediately Aeneas got up. All those who lived in Lydda and Sharon saw him and turned to the Lord.
-Acts 9:32-35

Aeneas probably had no idea if he would ever walk. What would have been the chances of him ever walking after being paralyzed for eight years? It wouldn't happen by chance but only by the power of God.

Death of Tabitha:
In Joppa there was a disciple named Tabitha (in Greek her name is Dorcas); she was always doing good and helping the poor. About that time she became sick and died, and her body was washed and placed in an upstairs room. Lydda was near Joppa; so when the disciples heard that Peter was in Lydda, they sent two men to him and urged him, "Please come at once!" Peter went with them, and when he arrived he was taken upstairs to the room. All the widows stood around him, crying and showing him the robes and other clothing that Dorcas had made while she was still with them. Peter sent them all out of the room; then he got down on his knees and prayed. Turning toward the dead woman, he said, "Tabitha, get up." She opened her eyes, and seeing Peter she sat up. He took her by the hand and helped her to her feet. Then he called for the believers, especially the widows,

and presented her to them alive. This became known all over Joppa,
and many people believed in the Lord. Peter stayed in Joppa for some
time with a tanner named Simon.
-Acts 9:36-43

It wasn't her appointed time. Her death was temporary and caused many to believe in the Lord.

Conspiracy to Kill Saul:

...Saul spent several days with the disciples in Damascus. At once he
began to preach in the synagogues that Jesus is the Son of God. All
those who heard him were astonished and asked, "Isn't he the man
who raised havoc in Jerusalem among those who call on this
name? And hasn't he come here to take them as prisoners to the chief
priests?" Yet Saul grew more and more powerful and baffled the Jews
living in Damascus by proving that Jesus is the Messiah. After many
days had gone by, there was a conspiracy among the Jews to kill
him, but Saul learned of their plan. Day and night they kept close
watch on the city gates in order to kill him. But his followers took him
by night and lowered him in a basket through an opening in the wall.
- Acts 9:19-25

Think about these scriptures. Does it look like there is a hedge of protection around Saul?

You see, it isn't always what you think. I'm sure you have thought of times that you were glad for some closed doors. Closed doors can be a blessing.

When you're faced with a closed door – or the appearance of one – and you don't understand, talk (pray) to the Lord about it. He may be trying to tell you something. Don't try to open a door with your own power. This would be like a woman or man looking for a mate and not waiting on God's timing. They accept the first thing that comes along looking nice and saying the right thing. They later find they married the devil. This may sound funny, but you would be surprised at the number of people who have done just that. But you wouldn't do anything like this, right? I've heard women say they were looking for their husband or their Boaz. I tell them, "You don't have to look because he'll find you." Proverbs 18:22 says, "He who finds a wife finds what is good and receives favor from the Lord." Okay, all the single ladies wanting to be married, tell the Lord thank you. Now, allow God to direct him to you.

THE HOUSE NEXT DOOR

I have served in prison ministry for more than 35 years. Some leave incarceration with nowhere to go. They're homeless. This is one of the major barriers facing those who are released. Some have returned to their same unhealthy environments only to get back in trouble and go back to prison. I asked several of those who returned what happened. They said they had no stability and nowhere to go. Like other areas, there are few to no shelters for those leaving incarceration in our region. I wished there was a place for them, but what could I do?

One night as I was heading to the jail for Bible Study with the ladies, I noticed an empty house. The Lord spoke and said, "You've always wanted a place for the ladies to go when they get out." This sounded good, but how would it happen? This looked like a closed door.

I mentioned it to my husband. He said, "Lin, we don't have the money. But if you want to look into it, go ahead." Fred was right about our lack of money. We had plenty of bills and a daughter on her way to college. My daughter even commented, "Momma, how can you all try to get that house when you know I'm going to college?" She was right, but I heard the Lord and I figured He would have to work it out. This house would be a huge undertaking and in need of some major repairs.

So, we went through the doors. Time and time again a door would open and then close. Finally, one stayed open and God provided the resources. Other caring individuals saw and became involved in what we were doing for the glory of God.

What appeared to be a closed door was a door that God had already opened. We could have given up the first time the door was closed, but we kept moving forward. We turned the knob, weren't moved by our circumstances, and walked through the door.

PHYLLIS' DOOR

My family background is catholic. I have been raped. The first time I was 3. The next time I was raped at 5 and my mother would press charges.

My mother was addicted to men. The men only used her and that just made her meaner. She would beat me when one of her men friends would leave her. She said it was my fault.

She would come home at night and tell me to get out and not come back till morning. This started when I was 4 or 5 years old. I would crawl under my friend's porch and I would sleep with their dog. Sometimes my friend's parents would let me in their house and bathe me and let me sleep over.

My mother never showed me love. She said she always tried to kill me before I was born. She didn't know how to love me. She only wanted someone to love her. She would call me a whore or a slut, and say she wished I was dead.

I always went to school with my hair messed up and dirty. I would tell the other kids I liked it to be like that so no one would know I was ashamed or that no one cared or loved me. No one ever cared or checked on families back then. They just took the parent's word that everything was okay.

I kept getting raped till I was about 13. I had no one to protect me. I left home and moved in a rain sewer till I was 14. I still went to school. I got a waitress job. I worked after school and I finally got an apartment for $75 a month.

I have carried the hurt for over 30 years and even dream about it. I still feel the pain that seems to not fade. I would like it to get behind me. Lots of days I felt it would be better if I was dead for my sake and others. I still struggle with it today.

I don't know how to care about myself or love myself. I need peace; I have so many voices running circles in my head. I stay angry at times for days and don't know why I'm mad at everyone who comes in my path. I don't know if it's because of my past or if it's the way I deal with things so I don't have to feel the pain that runs my body down day after day. I pray and pray for God's help and understanding, but I seem to end up right back at the pain of hurt, disappointment, anger, and dreams of being abused repeatedly.

I don't really know how to love or take care of another person because there was always a cost. I have two children but they don't live with me. I failed them as a mother as my mother did me. I just want to be free of hurt to love my children as a real mother. I have become the coldest person when all my children ever wanted was for me to love them. I do love them, but have only done so from afar. My son died, so he'll never know love from me and I'll never be able to show or give it to him. I feel I killed my own son. Every day I hate myself for the pain I must have caused him for not being his mother. I have a daughter who I want to have a good relationship with, but I constantly let her down. Please, Lord, help me to love my child, for I need to do something right for my child and me. Please help me, Jesus, to face this inner self pain that tears me up inside day and night. I feel I'm about to crack. I feel myself losing my grip...help me.

I forgive my mom, my stepfather, her men friends, the people who hurt and abused me, and the three men who raped me eight years ago who left me for dead. And I forgive myself.

NOTE: *We received this letter from Phyllis. Phyllis is no longer with us as she was involved in a fatal car accident. Although she experienced several closed doors while on this earth, she was able to experience freedom through Christ Jesus before her death.*

OPENED DOORS

"Come in, the door is open." This is what I say when I hear a knock or the doorbell ring at my door. If the door is locked, I go and unlock it. However, if I don't want to be bothered, I don't respond. How do you respond when there's a knock or doorbell ring at your door? One way or the other, even if it's no response, we make a choice. But for today, let's observe in this chapter how we should respond to open doors.

I picture an open door as being given access or an invitation to something. It reminds me of Jesus standing at the door and knocking. He said, "If anyone hears my voice and opens the door, I will come in and eat with that person, and they with me" (Revelation 3:20). We also get an invitation to life or death:

See, I set before you today life and prosperity, death and destruction. For I command you today to love the LORD your God, to walk in obedience to him, and to keep his commands, decrees and laws; then you will live and increase, and the LORD your God will bless you in the land you are entering to possess.
-Deuteronomy 30:15-16

You see, an open door shows that there's a way out and can also provide a view of what lies ahead; an open door is not closed or blocked up. An open door can also be defined as a door of opportunities that leads to your success. Proverbs 4:18 says, "The path of the righteous is like the morning sun, shining ever brighter till the full light of day." Jeremiah 29:11 says, "For I know the plans I have for you...plans to prosper you and not to harm you, plans to give you hope and a future."

As encouraging as the scriptures are when they tell us about open doors, we actually get to choose how we see an open door.

A NEW BEGINNING

We may not see the open door as a new beginning because we're reluctant or afraid to enter because of past experiences. We're stuck in pain or feelings of rejection, abuse, hurt, anxiety, worry, loss, compromise, inadequacy or unworthiness. I get it. You and I aren't the only ones who have stood at open doors.

I encourage you to choose to believe that an open door can be a symbol of a new beginning. God opened a door and told Abraham to go to a land He would show him. Abraham left familiarity for a place he had never been (Genesis 12:1). In the same way, God told Moses to go and bring the Israelites out of Egypt (Exodus 3:10). Surely, God knew Moses was on the run from Egypt. Here's another: Jesus told the rich young ruler to go, sell everything he had, give to the poor, and then come follow him. There stood an open door but the ruler did not walk through it (Mark 10:21-22). And, Jesus told the disciples to go into all the world and preach the gospel (Matthew 28:19-20). All the world can almost sound impossible. But God!

God set an open door before King Cyrus, a man that didn't know or serve Him. The open door let the world know—including those not serving Him – that God is God:

"This is what the LORD says to his anointed,
   to Cyrus, whose right hand I take hold of
to subdue nations before him
   and to strip kings of their armor,
to open doors before him
   so that gates will not be shut:
I will go before you
   and will level the mountains;
I will break down gates of bronze
   and cut through bars of iron.
I will give you hidden treasures,
   riches stored in secret places,
so that you may know that I am the LORD
the God of Israel, who summons you by name.

For the sake of Jacob my servant,
  of Israel my chosen,
I summon you by name
  and bestow on you a title of honor,
  though you do not acknowledge me.
I am the LORD, and there is no other;
  apart from me there is no God.
I will strengthen you,
  though you have not acknowledged me,
so that from the rising of the sun
  to the place of its setting
people may know there is none besides me.
  I am the LORD, and there is no other.
I form the light and create darkness,
  I bring prosperity and create disaster;
  I, the LORD, do all these things.
-Isaiah 45:1-7

Yes, God can open a door and use anyone to accomplish His will. Even you and me. We just have to trust Him and walk through the door.

I went through an open door I had never gone through before when doctors said I had a cancer called non-Hodgkin's Lymphoma in 2007. I was minding my own business and serving the Lord when told I had non-Hodgkin's lymphoma. Cancer doesn't sound like an open door, does it? The recommended treatment was six rounds of chemotherapy. I remembered the word the Lord had spoken to me and I wasn't being moved by what I was hearing, so I stopped after the second treatment. Even though I was given a survival rate of approximately 30%, I was willing to die for what I believed. I know and have a personal relationship with the Owner of the open door. I went through this door, not leaning to my own understanding, and trusting the Lord. I took Him at His Word:

Ask and it will be given to you; seek and you will find; knock and the door will be opened to you. For everyone who asks receives; the one who seeks finds; and to the one who knocks, the door will be opened.
-Matthew 7:7-8

I searched the scriptures and found promises for healing, peace, and provision. I share some of them at the back of this book. I lost my hair and now walk around in alopecia form. I haven't tried to figure that out, either, but if I wanted some more hair, I could buy it in all shapes and colors. What I have figured out is this: I'm glorifying God with this open door: I'm sharing the Gospel and letting others know that He still heals and to not give up. It's an open door that others are being encouraged by. You can find out more of how I walked through this door in our first book, *You Have To Be Willing To Die.* Check it out.

The door to your healing, freedom, peace, love, and joy is open, and Jesus has invited us to come in. We don't have to stand outside the door. We won't be alone because He will walk with us. This door stays open 24/7. We can come and go as we please. Jesus said, "I am the gate; whoever enters through me will be saved. They will come in and go out, and find pasture" (John 10:9). We find everything we need inside God's open doors. And I mean everything:

For no matter how many promises God has made, they are "Yes" in Christ. And so through him the "Amen" is spoken by us to the glory of God.
-2 Corinthians 1:20

The only one able to keep you from coming inside an open door for a new beginning is you. You have to exercise faith to walk through the open door. Stay in the Word of God and in tune with His leading. Not doing so could cause you to miss out on what He has waiting for you. Stop trying to figure things out. Just trust Him. Proverbs 3:5-6 says:

Trust in the LORD *with all your heart*
   and lean not on your own understanding;
in all your ways submit to him,
   and he will make your paths straight.

BUMPS IN THE ROAD

An open door is not always without some bumps (opposition/more doors) in the road. A door with a new beginning was opened for Saul, who would later be called Paul. Read Acts 9:1-9:

Meanwhile, Saul was still breathing out murderous threats against the Lord's disciples. He went to the high priest and asked him for letters to the synagogues in Damascus, so that if he found any there who belonged to the Way, whether men or women, he might take them as prisoners to Jerusalem. As he neared Damascus on his journey, suddenly a light from heaven flashed around him. He fell to the ground and heard a voice say to him, "Saul, Saul, why do you persecute me?"
"Who are you, Lord?" Saul asked.
"I am Jesus, whom you are persecuting," he replied. "Now get up and go into the city, and you will be told what you must do."
The men traveling with Saul stood there speechless; they heard the sound but did not see anyone. Saul got up from the ground, but when he opened his eyes he could see nothing. So they led him by the hand into Damascus. For three days he was blind, and did not eat or drink anything.

It's a new day — a new beginning. God stopped Saul right in his tracks. You may ask how is Saul's encounter a new beginning when Saul was blind and not eating or drinking anything. Remember, God opened the door. The Lord visited Ananias in a vision. He was to go and place his hands on Saul and restore his sight. Ananias heard of Saul and knew he was coming to arrest all who called on the Lord's name (Acts 9:10-14). The Lord said:

...Ananias, "Go! This man is my chosen instrument to proclaim my name to the Gentiles and their kings and to the people of Israel. I will show him how much he must suffer for my name."
-Acts 9:15-16

Saul was now off on his new beginning of an open door. He would proclaim the name of the Lord to the Gentiles and their kings and the people of Israel. And as he suffered, he experienced some bumps in the road.

Travel with me to Acts 14. Here's my short version: Paul and Barnabas are going – as usual – to the Jewish synagogue. A great number of Jews and Greeks believed in Jesus because of their message. Jews who refused to believe stirred up the other Gentiles and poisoned their minds against them. They were divided; some with the Jews, others with the apostles. Paul and Barnabas stayed there, speaking boldly for the Lord, with signs and wonders following.

There was a plot to mistreat Paul and Barnabas and stone them. The two found out about it and fled to Lystra and Derbe and to the surrounding country, where they continued to preach the gospel.

In Lystra, there sat a man who was lame from birth and had never walked. He listened to Paul as he was speaking. Paul looked directly at him, saw that he had faith to be healed, and called out, "Stand up on your feet!" At that, the man jumped up and began to walk.

The crowd saw it and said the gods had come down in human form. Paul and Barnabas let the people know they were human, like themselves, bringing the good news to turn from worthless things to the living God.

Still, some Jews came from Antioch and Iconium and won the crowd over. They stoned Paul and dragged him outside the city, thinking he was dead. But after the disciples had gathered around him, he got up and went back into the city. The next day Paul and Barnabas left for Derbe. They preached the gospel in that city and won a large number of disciples.

Then they returned to Lystra, Iconium, and Antioch, strengthening the disciples and encouraging them to remain true to the faith. They told them how God had opened a door of faith to the Gentiles. "We must go through many hardships to enter the kingdom of God," they said.

Let's pause for a moment (like for gas or a quick potty break) and talk about some of the things we noticed on the trip.

Pause Break – Pause Break!

Did you notice the "bumps" – or the plot – to mistreat Paul and Barnabas? First, Paul and Barnabus were minding their own business. They were doing what they usually do by going to the synagogue. Then there was some division, but that's to be expected when the truth is told. They stoned Paul and dragged him outside the city, thinking he was dead. But you can't stop the Gospel from being preached. Through it all, the door remained open, Jesus was preached, many came to the Lord, and signs and wonders followed, to include the man who had never walked (Acts 14:8-10).

So, you can expect some bumps. Just stay the course and let God handle them.

It seems that there were always bumps in the road for Saul (Paul) with preaching the Gospel. There was a conspiracy among the Jews to kill him and he learned about it. His followers took him by night and lowered him in a basket through an opening in the wall (Acts 9:23-25). Another time involved him being under house arrest in Jerusalem (Acts 28). He remained incarcerated until appealing to Caesar in order to avoid an assassination attempt. He could not leave or travel freely. You see, the door wasn't closed because Paul continued to preach the Gospel. While awaiting trial in Rome, he wrote in Colossians:

And pray for us, too, that God may open a door for our message, so
that we may proclaim the mystery of Christ, for which I am in chains.
-Colossians 4:3

Pause Break – Pause Break!

Did you notice that in all of the bumps in the road, Paul did not
ask the saints to pray for his freedom? Instead, he asked them
to petition God for opportunities to share the Gospel. Paul was
on a mission and about the Lord's business of spreading the
message of Christ, regardless of the cost.

Do you think the average Christian would have responded in
this manner having gone through what Paul experienced?
What about you?

Paul also spoke of other open doors for preaching in 1
Corinthians 16:9 and 2 Corinthians 2:12. Here are two more
scriptures:

because a great door for effective work has opened to me, and there are
many who oppose me.
-1 Corinthians 16:9

Now when I went to Troas to preach the gospel of Christ and found
that the Lord had opened a door for me,
-2 Corinthians 2:12

Are you like Paul, willing to stay the course, even if it kills you?

I HAVE TO TELL YOU SOMETHING

Do you remember hearing, "I have to tell you something"?
Most of the time it was a secret, right? Well, I have to tell you
something and it's no secret. God also closes doors that you

want open or that He once opened for you for a season. So, don't get discouraged if a door you hoped would open has remained shut or a door has recently shut in your life. It could be something God does not want for you and has therefore shut the door. You and I know that we have some doors that need to be shut. The beauty is that God has something even better in store. He has an open door prepared just for you that will bring His best for your life.

In Revelation 3:7 we read: "To the angel of the church in Philadelphia write: These are the words of him who is holy and true, who holds the key of David. What he opens no one can shut, and what he shuts no one can open." John received this revelation from God while exiled on the Isle of Patmos. In this scripture, the One who is holy and true, the One who has the key of David refers to Jesus. Jesus can open doors no one can close, and close doors no one can open. Jesus holds the keys. Whatever He opens and closes is the will of God.

What doors do you sense God is opening for you? Do you have apprehensions, or, are you afraid to enter? Go to Him in prayer and listen for His voice. Ask Him for confirmation. I can tell you that if it doesn't line up with scripture, then it's not from God.

You have another door outside of the physical realm that God is knocking on, too. It's your heart. Have you opened it to Him? If not, He is waiting for you to open the door and let Him in. As I always say, your life will never be the same. Let Him in. God opens and will lead us through the doors He wants us to walk through. If we delight in Him, He will make our steps firm (Psalm 37:23).

LINDA'S DOOR

I am a woman who was never loved by her Dad. I wanted him to love me. I was his daughter. So, I looked for love in all the wrong places, starting at a young age. I got involved with different men thinking they would love me. They said they would love me but it always turned out to be lies. I gave myself to them, but they did not give themselves to me. These relationships were with married men who promised to leave their wives. They didn't. I can't say they took advantage of me. I allowed it. This was my life for 12 to 14 years.

After going through all that, another man began to pursue me. He was single. He said he wanted a relationship with me. We dated and eventually married. The courtship and marriage were abusive. He didn't physically beat me, but he was verbally abusive. I stayed in the marriage because I was determined it wasn't going to end. I would learn years later that he had made a bet with other guys that he would get me.

I gave my life to the Lord and received the baptism of the Holy Spirit during the marriage. I began to intercede for him. After 12 years in the marriage, my husband died. Our marriage was not the way it should have been between a husband and wife, but I wouldn't take anything for that journey. It has helped me in so many ways.

Fast forward to 2020 and we're in a pandemic. I took advantage of it and spent a lot of time with the Lord. He continued to work on me. I had to own my portion in my marriage because I had brought some baggage into it. I wasn't healed from previous relationships. God revealed to me that the men could only do what they did because I allowed it to happen. God has done a wonder in my life.

I sometimes compare my life with Leah in the Bible. Her dad gave her to a man (Jacob) that didn't want her. He didn't even love her. She didn't have a choice in the matter. She had to go and lay with him. I've often wondered if he loved his daughter and if Leah felt love from her father. I could relate from this standpoint because I did not have love from a father. I entered into relationships looking for love. There Leah was in a loveless marriage with Jacob and having babies. Having baby after baby didn't appear to make him love her. He wanted someone else: her sister, Rachel. Rachel was the one he fell in love with and had been promised. I could identify with that, too, because there were other women in our relationship.

Then, Leah had a fourth child and named him Judah, which means praise. She stopped having children and I believe she stopped trying to get her husband's attention.

I believe God saw that Leah wasn't loved. I loved my husband but he didn't love me as his wife. But God loved me and still does. Even though I went through a lot of pain, disappointment, and hurt, I always clung to hope. I never lost it. He kept me. Just like the meaning of Judah's name, I always had a praise. I always had a worship. That was my go-to. I stand strong today because God loves me. Greatness came out of Leah even with so much against her. I, too, already had so much against me. Greatness has and continues to come into my life. I am favored by the Lord. I am approved by the Lord. It's morning time. It's morning in my life!

God saw me polluted. He didn't just let me lay there. He didn't leave me in the state I was in. He saw me. He covered me in His love. He began to clothe me with his Word. He fed me the best of the best, the Gospel. He did that for me. He's building my character. And now, I'm ministry-ready. I am in a position to tell my story to help somebody. I'm still here. To God be the glory. I submit to the process. I yield all my emotions to the Lord. Everything I am and not, I belong to Jesus. I'm excited about this life I now live. I made some wrong decisions and I own them. But God was there all the time. I say He had me hemmed in like Psalm 139. He saw me, He spoke over me, He acknowledged me, He covered me, He promised me, He cleansed me, He dressed me, He fed me, and now He's establishing me for His glory! All things are new. He has always loved me, and He loves you. This is an open door for me and I'm submitting to the process. And you can, too.

The door is open.

AMANDA'S DOOR

I am a single mom of four. I struggled with addiction for 14 years. I am a four-time felon and a former inmate. This is my story.

I come from a great family with a wonderful childhood. Both parents were involved in my life and are still married to this day. I got pregnant in high school with my first son at the age of 16. I continued with high school and made good grades. I graduated with dreams and hopes of going to college for nursing. On my 18th birthday, everything changed. My friends threw me a party and that is where I was introduced to meth. That one time is all it took for me to become hooked. It would take years before my family had a clue anything was going on. I was working two jobs at one point, going to nursing school, and being a mother to my son. Eventually, the addiction completely took over. I began putting friends and drugs ahead of my child. I dropped out of nursing school to pursue partying and to feed my addiction. The longer I used, the more I was hurting my family. They did not even recognize me anymore. I was stealing, lying, and pushing them as far away as possible. As long as I was feeding the addiction, nothing else mattered to me.

After years of just using, I decided to graduate to the next level and start selling. It started small and then quickly jumped to bigger payouts with more drugs. Fast forward to 2009, I finally got payouts with even more drugs and was arrested for the first time. In 2010, I was charged with trafficking meth and sentenced to 15 years. I was mad, ashamed, hated myself, and thought my life was over. I was able to accept a plea deal all due to something going wrong with my co-defendant's trial (which usually doesn't happen) and was sent to the work release facility for one year. I was mad and did not understand why this was happening to me. I wasn't hurting anybody but myself, right? The first weekend at work release, I met Mrs. Linda Wimes. My roommate convinced me to go to church with her. I was uncomfortable and felt out of place. I hadn't been to church since I was a little girl. I didn't understand why she was wasting her time on an addict like me.

While sitting in church, something happened. Something changed. I began to cry and pray. I felt a pull like I never have before. I walked to the front of the church and gave my life to the Lord. I remember after church that day Mrs. Linda took everyone else back to the work release but me. She sat me down and told me that God had a calling on my life. She didn't know what it was, but she knew it was special. We talked for what seemed like hours and then she took me back. I worked with her and her ministry that entire year. She answered all my questions about Jesus and treated me like a person. She trusted me. She accepted me. I know now that the time with Mrs. Linda was something I was craving since I'd forced my family to lose trust in me. I gained so much head knowledge about Jesus. However, at the time, I never let it profoundly change my heart.

I was released from work release in October 2011. I was sober for the first time in years, and it felt great! I wanted to share this newfound freedom with my old "friends". I wanted to save them. I stopped listening to God's leading and did what I wanted to do. Within a few months, I was not only using but I was selling again. By June of 2012, I was pregnant. I ran the roads selling while pregnant and saw nothing wrong with it. That's one of the terrible things about addiction. It blinds you before you start dealing with feelings of shame again - ashamed of getting right back into what I fought so hard to get away from. So, instead of asking for help or talking about how I was feeling, I began to push away the ones that I love the most again to try to hide what I was doing. This time, they weren't falling for it. They knew. They were heartbroken, but I didn't care.

By October of 2012, I was arrested yet again. I was able to only spend one night and bond out. After I got out, I promised myself I would change, and that I could do it on my own. I didn't ask for help or talk about it because I was embarrassed. I hid it all inside and acted as if I had it together. In January of 2013, my beautiful son was born. I knew at that moment I needed to get it together for him and his brother. I could do this! Notice I said for him and his brother, not for me. I didn't change much. I kept hanging out with some old "friends" and by March of 2013, I was back in jail. This time I stayed in for eight months just waiting on a court date. That rarely happens. Most people have a court date within a couple of months. I look back now and know that this was God trying to sit me down.

I finally got home and everything – again – was great! My family attempted trusting me again. I was trying so hard. I knew I could do it for them this time. Again, for them. Not me. I tried to do it on my own again because I was strong enough, right? Wrong! Within five months, the police kicked the door in at my parent's house for me and arrested me in front of my dad and son. This was it. My family was done. I bonded out and went on the run because they did not want me at their house anymore. I knew that this time I would go to prison and I was more willing to live a life hiding than to face the truth. While on the run, I got pregnant again. I remember being so scared and wanting to turn myself in, but I just couldn't. I didn't want to have my baby in prison, so I came up with a plan. After I had my child, I would turn myself in and face the truth. I didn't get that chance. The police found me, and I was arrested at five months pregnant. I know this sounds crazy, but it was such a relief. I was so tired of running. I slept better that night than I had in years. It was finally over.

I went to prison and had my third son in February of 2015. I was able to spend two nights with him at the hospital before I had to leave him there and return to my punishment. I remember staying up the entire 48 hours talking to him so he would remember my voice. I told him how sorry I was and that he would love his grandparents and brothers. That I would see him soon, but that mommy had to get better first. On the way back to prison, I cried out to God. I asked Him to please not let me leave prison until I was the woman He made me to be. I wanted every old person, place, and thing removed from my life and replaced with things of Him and people who absolutely loved Jesus.

In December of 2015, I was able to transfer back to the work release where I started so many years ago. But this time I was different. This time all that head knowledge I had before was being put into action. I didn't just know about Jesus, I knew Him. I had a relationship with Him like never before. Not only did I know who He was; I knew who I was in Him. I trusted

Him more than ever.

I got home and knew that things would be hard with my family, especially my oldest son. He was now 17 and hurt. He didn't trust me, and I didn't blame him. I didn't push. I trusted God. I allowed the change in me to shine through my actions. I stayed focused on Jesus and I prayed. My son wouldn't even speak to me for a long time. I could be standing right next to him and he would act like I wasn't even there. Did it hurt? Absolutely! Did I give up? Never! I stood strong on God's promises. When the enemy would whisper in my ear things like, "That door is closed. Give up!" I would yell back Joel 2:25, "The Lord says, 'I will give you back what you lost....'" I would speak the truth over my family and again trusted God. I allowed my life and actions to speak for me.

Now, my relationship with my family is better than it has ever been. My oldest son is my friend, and we talk daily. There isn't a day that goes by that we don't say we love each other. My family trusts me and it's great! I have an amazing church home and a wonderful small group. I can look back at my story and see so many times that God was just waiting on me to walk through the open door. It was the door that He so desperately wanted me to enter, but He never forced me. He never left me, even when I left Him.

My prayer is that in reading my story you see that God is there. He is waiting patiently for you to walk through that open door and find out who you are in Him.

My name is Amanda. I am a mother to four beautiful children. I have been sober for over six years! I speak the truth to help others struggling with addiction and to let them know that they are not alone. I am confident. I am loved. I am redeemed. This is my story.

REBECCA'S DOOR

Addiction impacts every life, everywhere, in one way or another. I was not prepared to be a mother of a child who would battle drug addiction for over 10 years. I was not the person with the drug addiction, but it became mine because I allowed myself to take ownership of it. As parents, we are always looking and searching for ways to fix our broken children. However, this was not the battle in which I wanted to be.

Working with mental illness and addiction is my profession. I was trained in this area so I knew what to do. As parents in the mental health career field, we always say "I hope this never hits home," but it did. I didn't see it coming. He wasn't raised like that. Was I clueless or naïve to the fact that this disease could not attack my child, or was I exempt from this horrible nightmare? Here's a wake-up call: drug addiction is a disease that hits all types of families. No one is excluded.

James was a good kid, very active in school sports, and a very well-mannered young man. He loved his family and loved helping others. His compassion was toward the homeless and the less fortunate. James would always find someone that needed food or a place to sleep. He brought them home to feed them. I never knew what to expect. At age 21, James married his high school sweetheart and they had a beautiful baby boy, although their marriage didn't last long. Somewhere down the line, James began to spiral deeper and deeper into drugs in hopes it would ease his pain. He would always tell me he had it under control, but the drugs were the ones in control. At this point, he was spending most of his time in and out of jail. James would call every time begging to be bailed out with promises that he would change and stop doing drugs. So, what would I do? I would bail him out every time, hoping and believing he wanted to change.

James became very good at manipulation to get what he wanted. This went on for a while. He'd play on my emotions and made me feel guilty as though I didn't care about him.

At one point, I was done making excuses for his hurtful and destructive behavior, but I maintained compassion for him because I knew his story all too well.

I became co-dependent and responsible for the action of his addiction in an attempt to keep him safe. I allowed James to stay in my home even if he was using drugs. I lied to family and friends to create excuses that defended his addictive behavior. I was good about shifting blame onto other people rather than him. To me, my intentions were good in wanting to keep him safe, but I never allowed James to take or face any consequences of his choices in his addictive behavior. I was only prolonging the suffering of both him and myself that he would endure. Without consequences, there was no incentive for James to stop doing drugs.

Seeing James endure the side effects of drugs and the rage that it brought upon him broke my heart. He was unrecognizable to the point that I did not know him anymore. His physical appearance was nothing to be desired with the long hair and long beard. He reminded me of the movie, Cast Away, with Tom Hanks where he was left on an island to survive four years of misery. James' behavior and thought process was not the same.

You may think you are alone in sharing someone's addiction or your own, and often physically, you are, but emotionally you are not. The effects are shared. I hid what I was feeling and I hid the truth from those around me. I suffered the shame and I carried the blame. I know this is not about me, but I knew I never saw it coming, and if I had, I would have done anything to stop it.

As I reflect on the last 10 years of James's addiction, the hardest thing was I could not separate his addiction from my son himself. I just couldn't see past it. My hurt and anger toward him would move me to do things I'm not proud of. I would scream and say hurtful things to him, blaming him for taking away the relationship I so desired to have with him as mother and son. I cannot pretend to understand what the addiction has put him through, but I can see what it has taken from him in so many ways. Addiction can leave you feeling overwhelmed with thoughts of confusion, loneliness, anger, and fear. God is not a bit surprised by our trials and sufferings, because pain is not without purpose. I can see that pain can, however, be used for our good as part of God's work.

It was through my son's brokenness where I found a much deeper and more compassionate, loving relationship with God. I have found peace by resting in God's presence and knowing Romans 8:28: "And we know that in all things God works for the good of those who love him, who have been called according to his purpose."

Today, James and I are in a much better place in our relationship. It's not where I would like it to be, but it is where God has us. Letting go has not been easy for me but through the grace of God, we are moving forward and not backward. I had to surrender it all to God and trust Him with it all.

Little by little, we see victory every day. You see, I walk by faith even when I cannot see.

I wanted hope. I wanted something to happen that would bring changes to our situation and circumstances. I found myself lost and not knowing what to do or where to seek help and guidance. Deep down, I knew and had forgotten my profession. Here are two resources that I found helpful: Setting Boundaries with Your Adult Children by Allison Bottke and Boundaries: When to Say Yes, When to Say No by Drs. Henry Cloud and John Townsend.

Sarah Young in Jesus Calling says, "When you release loved ones to Me, you are free to cling to My hand. As you entrust others into My care, I am free to shower blessings on them. My presence will go with them wherever they go, and I will give them rest. This same presence stays with you. As you relax and place your trust in Me. Watch to see what I will do. JUST DON'T GIVE UP."

Paul says in Philippians 4:6-7, "Don't worry about anything; instead, pray about everything. Tell God what you need, and thank him for all he has done" (NLT).

Surrender it all and let God have His way.

MY RECENT DOOR

I was faced with an unexpected door while writing this book. I went for my annual mammogram breast screening on March 1,

2021. I normally receive the results in a text message the same day, but not so this time. I wondered why I hadn't received it and assumed the office was just busy. It would be two days later before receiving the message:

The assessment was not readily classified as benign, additional reviews are recommended.

A door and a choice to make. I could cry, worry, or lose it. My life experiences with the doors I've faced taught me to tell my situation to the One who really knows what's going on and can do something about it. So, I held my phone up towards heaven. "God, do you see what they're saying?" I asked.

I felt in my spirit God replying, "It's not cancer."

That was it. I went on about my business. I later received a call from my doctor's office informing me to expect a call to schedule an appointment for additional reviews. I did not tell anyone else what was going on at this time – only the Lord. The next call came:

"Hello Southeast Health," I said. (Hint: I don't have ESP but their number is programmed in my phone.)

"May I speak to Linda Wimes?"

"This is Linda Wimes. I was expecting your call. When would you like for me to bring my right breast back to you?"

"Is this Linda Wimes?" she asked again.

"Yes, it is."

"I've never called and received such a response," she said.

"This is nothing," I replied. "When would you like me to come?"

An appointment was scheduled for a week later. At this time, I informed my husband and daughter, Fred and Christi, while laughing about what was going on. I was at peace and my faith was intact because I had told God and received an answer. This was about to be another opportunity for God to be glorified. Fred and Christi agreed and laughed with me. I waited in anticipation of my appointment. I call these the what-if moments: What if it's cancer? What if it's not? Still, I remembered what the Lord had spoken and kept moving right along. You see, I have learned that God will use whatever door we face to show Himself strong in our lives.

I arrived at my appointment on March 9, 2021. I met the young lady who called to schedule the appointment. I had the opportunity to share with her about the goodness of the Lord and how He healed me of non-Hodgkin's lymphoma. She explained more about how my response to her call was not typical of what she receives. We had a great conversation and were both encouraged.

When the screening was completed and reviewed, the doctor arrived and said, "Mrs. Wimes, we have good news. I don't see anything, not even what was there before. We'll see you in a year."

Of course, this was great news, but this appointment was something so much bigger than the assessment not readily classified as benign. This appointment was an open door. It turned out for good and was an answer to a prayer we had prayed in December 2020 to get a copy of our first book, *You Have To Be Willing To Die: Don't Be Moved By What You Hear*, into the Women's Center so that it could be shared with others who needed to be encouraged as they visited there for various reasons. Although I didn't know how this would happen, God knew, and it worked out that I had the opportunity to share three books and testify about my awesome God. You see, what seemed like a bump in the road was an open door, which resulted in me making a choice, and God being glorified. It doesn't get any better.

----------------CONCLUSION----------------

As we said in our Introduction, doors are everywhere. They may cause some uncertainties to surface on the inside of us. No one can shut down the inner fears and deepest agonies that you're facing. But there is one, the Lord, who is willing to help you face them. He does this as you yield and have faith in Him.

Where there's a door, we face a choice, and at the end of the day, the choice is yours and yours alone. No one can make it for you. What action will you take? Will you see it as an opportunity to be set free? Will you push forward or be defeated by the barrier? What if the door is one that caused or causes you pain, discomfort, or anguish? Will you have hope? Will you face the door and say as Joseph did to his brothers in Genesis 50:20: "You intended to harm me, but God intended it for good to accomplish what is now being done, the saving of many lives"?

You are the apple of God's eye. To be the apple of someone's eye means that you are being gazed upon and watched closely by that person. Now – just like Joseph – this doesn't mean you will not encounter some challenging doors. Did you notice that for a while, every time something positive was happening for Joseph, it was soon replaced with something negative? And God was with, watching over, and giving Joseph favor the whole time. He was never alone. And you aren't, either.

As we have traveled through Joseph's life in scripture in this book, we can see that the doors he faced were part of his training to get him to the place God had for him: the palace. Think about it. He learned about the Egyptian people and their language. He acquired management skills that taught him how to run a successful Fortune 500 business. He learned to interact with all kinds of people, including the deceitful, forgetful, and liars. I'm not sure if Joseph would have learned all of these things while tending his father's flock. Do you think that all he went through was a bad trade-off to end up as second-in-command in charge of the whole land of Egypt? Could it be the doors you face are preparing you for the place the Lord has prepared for you, as well?

Joseph's journey to his position in the palace didn't happen overnight. Nor will it be for us. He experienced loss. He lost his mother at an early age and the comfort and privileges of being with his beloved father. He lost his freedom and became a slave and eventually a prisoner. He would not see his father again until he was probably 41 years old. Joseph was tried and tested, and we will be, too. Joseph passed the test and we can, too. But only if we do what Joseph did. Although he was in a foreign land, Joseph remained faithful and consistent, and his character remained the same. There are no shortcuts.

Although we may not understand their purpose, know that God is using doors in your life for your good and for His glory. As a child of God, your future is bright, but you must contend for it by faith. This is because the enemy doesn't want you to have an abundant life. The fight is on. We are told in scriptures to fight the fight of faith, and in 1 John 5:4, we are told that our faith is what gives us the victory. Do not be afraid to face your doors because God is for you and will be with you every step of the way. As a matter of fact, He's already been where you're going. Remember, He knows everything (1 John 3:20). And check this out: not only does He know everything, but no weapon that is formed against you shall prosper (Isaiah 54:17).

God isn't surprised about the doors you face or your decisions. Just like Joseph, we're in training for something far better than we can see right now. Staying before the Lord will teach you how to live one day at a time, despite the doors of sorrow, tears, and pain. You will learn how to rejoice in the Lord, no matter what happens.

Those who shared their testimonies in this book are living witnesses that you can make it. Will it seem hard at times? Yes. Will you feel like you want to give up? Yes. But, don't quit or give in. I feel about you just like our Heavenly Father does: You are a Winner. You are an Overcomer. Now, you say it, too. Say it out loud: Who Are You?

When the fog surrounds you and you can't see past your doors, rest in the arms of Jesus and simply trust Him. Should you have a setback, see it as your next move forward. Remain faithful and God will do for you what He did for Joseph. He is no respecter of persons (Acts 10:34). Remember, God has good thoughts toward you and a perfect plan for your life (Jeremiah 29:11).

Let's pray together:

Lord, we are faced with many doors and many times we don't know what to do. We have to make choices and sometimes we're afraid that we may make the wrong choice. But Lord, we're going to be like Jehoshaphat in the Bible and look to you. May our hearts be opened to hear you and take you at your Word. Lord, help us to know that we can trust you at all times. We can trust knowing that you are with us, every step of the way.

Lord, we thank you for your protection as we face our doors. Our excuses of present and past disappointments, failures, insecurities, loss, and all the other excuses we've claimed will not hinder us from facing and walking through the doors that are placed before us. We will not compromise or walk in unforgiveness. Instead, we will keep our hearts pure before you. We place our hope and faith in you because we know we will not be disappointed. Our lives are in your hands and available to be used for our good and your glory.

We love you!

SOURCES

[1]Altein, Yehuda. *Jewish History Biographies In Brief. The Story of Joseph in the Bible From Prisoner to Prince.*
https://www.chabad.org/library/article_cdo/aid/143035/je
wish/%20The-Story-of-Joseph-in-the-B%e2%80%a6

[2]Hopkins Medicine. *The Power of positive thinking.*
https://www.hopkinsmedicine.org/health/wellness-and-
prevention/the-power-of-positive-thinking

[3]Centers for Disease Control and Prevention. *Heart Disease.*
https://www.cdc.gov/heartdisease/about.htm

[4]American Heart Association. Is Broken Heart Syndrome
Real? https://www.heart.org/en/health-
topics/cardiomyopathy/what-is-cardiomyopathy-in-
adults/is-broken-heart-syndrome-real

[5]Centers for Disease Control and Prevention. *Preventing Sexual Violence.*
https://www.cdc.gov/violenceprevention/pdf/sv/SV-
factsheet_508.pdf

[6]Johns Hopkins Medicine. *Forgiveness: Your Health Depends on it.*
https://www.hopkinsmedicine.org/health/wellness-and-
prevention/forgiveness-your-health-depends-on-it

[7]Christianity Today. (2013, September). *Forgiving the Man Who Murdered My Mom*
https://www.christianitytoday.com/ct/2013/september/for
giving-man-who-murdered-my-mom.html?start=1

[8]Shapiro, E; Emerson, A., McFann, Kristen. (2017, January 10). *Dylann Roof Sentenced to Death, 1st to Get Death Penalty for Federal Hate Crimes*. ABC News Network. https://abcnews.go.com/US/charleston-church-shooter-dylann-roof-sentenced-death/story?id=44674575

[9]Izadi, E. (2015, June 19). The powerful words of forgiveness delivered to Dylann Roof by victims' relatives. *The Washington Post* https://www.washingtonpost.com/news/post-nation/wp/2015/06/19/hate-wont-win-the-powerful-words-delivered-to-dylann-roof-by-victims-relatives/

[10]*Facing death for church shooting, Dylan Roof says: "I still feel like I had to do it"*. CBS News. Updated on: January 10, 017/3:58PM/CBS/AP https://www.cbsnews.com/news/dylann-roof-death-sentence-hearing-jury-deliberations/

[11]*Brandt Jean to Amber Guyger: 'I forgive you'*. ABC News Network. https://abcnews.go.com/US/video/brandt-jean-amber-guyger-forgive-66018935

[12]The Christian Chronicle. (October 13, 2019). *Guilty and Forgiven* https://christianchronicle.org/guilty-and-forgiven/

[13]Kuruvilla, C. (2019, October 08). *Texas Judge Defends Hugging, Gifting Bible To Bothan Jean's Killer*. https://www.huffpost.com/entry/tammy-kemp-defends-Bible_n_5d9ca61de4b03b475fa08623

[14]The Washington Informer. (October 11, 2019). *Interview: One-on-One with Judge Tammy Kemp from Amber Guyer Murder Trial* https://www.washingtoninformer.com/interview-one-on-one-with-judge-tammy-kemp-from-amber-guyger-murder-trial/

[15]Lewis B. Smedes Quotes
https://www.azquotes.com/author/13725-Lewis_B_Smedes

[16]Child Safe House Organization. *Why Do Children Not Tell.*
https://www.childsafehouse.org/info/faqs/why-do-children-not-tell/

RESOURCES

National hotlines can help connect victims, survivors, and their support networks connect with local resources.

Child Abuse
1-800-4-A-CHILD (1-800-422-4453)
The Childhelp National Child Abuse Hotline is dedicated to the prevention of child abuse. Serving the U.S. and Canada, the hotline is staffed 24 hours a day, 7 days a week with professional crisis counselors who — through interpreters — provide assistance in over 170 languages. The hotline offers crisis intervention, information, and referrals to thousands of emergency, social service, and support resources. All calls, texts and chats are confidential.

Sexual Assault
1 (800) 656-4673
Available 24 hours a day, 7 days a week via phone and online chat.

RAINN (Rape, Abuse & Incest National Network) is the nation's largest anti-sexual violence organization. RAINN created and operates the National Sexual Assault Hotline (800.656.HOPE, online.rainn.org y rainn.org/es) in partnership with more than 1,000 local sexual assault service providers across the country and operates the DoD Safe Helpline for the Department of Defense. RAINN also carries out programs to prevent sexual violence, help survivors, and ensure that perpetrators are brought to justice.

Human Trafficking
Hotline: 1-888-373-7888
Text: 233733

The National Human Trafficking Hotline is a national anti-trafficking hotline serving victims and survivors of human trafficking and the anti-trafficking community in the United States. The toll-free hotline is available to answer calls from anywhere in the country, 24 hours a day, 7 days a week, every day of the year in more than 200 languages.

Mental and/or Substance Use Disorders
Helpline, **1-800-662-HELP (4357)** or TTY: **1-800-487-4889**

SAMHSA's (Substance Abuse and Mental Health Administration) National Helpline is a free, confidential, 24/7, 365-day-a-year treatment referral and information service (in English and Spanish) for individuals and families facing mental and/or substance use disorders.

SAMHSA's National Helpline, **1-800-662-HELP (4357)**, (also known as the Treatment Referral Routing Service) or TTY: **1-800-487-4889** is a confidential, free, 24-hour-a-day, 365-day-a-year, information service, in English and Spanish, for individuals and family members facing mental and/or substance use disorders. This service provides referrals to local treatment facilities, support groups, and community-based organizations.

SCRIPTURES

"For the word of God is alive and active. Sharper than any double-edged sword, it penetrates even to dividing soul and spirit, joints and marrow; it judges the thoughts and attitudes of the heart.
-Hebrews 4:12

The following pages contain some scriptures that will hopefully lead you to seek other scriptures for yourself. Search the scriptures. Spend time meditating on them. They are life and health to our bones. They always point us to the right doors. They will point us to Jesus, the One who knows us by name. 2 Timothy 3:16 reminds us: All Scripture is God-breathed and is useful for teaching, rebuking, correcting and training in righteousness.

Find comfort and peace through Scripture that promises you hope and a future. Fear, worry and anxiety are all weapons of the enemy to keep us from experiencing the full life that God has for us. These emotions can overwhelm us and keep us paralyzed. You can be free from worry and anxiety by meditating on the Word and casting your cares upon Jesus.

We will face many doors but know that God has given His Word, which He hastens to perform. He wants us to put him into remembrance. He will do just what He says. And He will never compromise or contradict His Word.

SCRIPTURES ON THE HEART

As water reflects the face, so one's life reflects the heart.
-Proverbs 27:19

You will seek me and find me when you seek me with all your heart.
-Jeremiah 29:13

Create in me a pure heart, O God, and renew a steadfast spirit within me.
-Psalm 51:10

Let love and faithfulness never leave you; bind them around your neck, write them on the tablet of your heart. Then you will win favor and a good name in the sight of God and man.
-Proverbs 3:3-4

Jesus replied: 'Love the Lord your God with all your heart and with all your soul and with all your mind.'
-Matthew 22:37

Take delight in the Lord, and he will give you the desires of your heart.
-Psalm 37:4

My son, do not forget my teaching, but keep my commands in your heart, for they will prolong your life many years and bring you peace and prosperity.
-Proverbs 3:1-2

The wise in heart accept commands, but a chattering fool comes to ruin.
-Proverbs 10:8

Be strong and take heart, all you who hope in the Lord.
-Psalm 31:24

I seek you with all my heart; do not let me stray from your commands.
-Psalm 119:10

Blessed are those who keep his statutes and seek him with all their heart.
-Psalm 119:2

He heals the brokenhearted and binds up their wounds.
-Psalm 147:3

Blessed are the pure in heart, for they will see God.
-Matthew 5:8

Anxiety weighs down the heart, but a kind word cheers it up.
-Proverbs 12:25

But I trust in your unfailing love; my heart rejoices in your salvation. I will sing the Lord's praise, for he has been good to me.
-Psalm 13:5-6

I have hidden your word in my heart that I might not sin against you.
-Psalm 119:11

Turn my heart toward your statutes and not toward selfish gain.
-Psalm 119:36

My son, pay attention to what I say; turn your ear to my words. Do not let them out of your sight, keep them within your heart.
-Proverbs 4:20-21

My son, if your heart is wise, then my heart will be glad indeed.
-Proverbs 23:15

Though an army besiege me, my heart will not fear; though war break out against me, even then I will be confident.
-Psalm 27:3

The precepts of the Lord are right, giving joy to the heart. The commands of the Lord are radiant, giving light to the eyes.
-Psalm 19:8

SCRIPTURES ON UNFORGIVENESS

for all have sinned and fall short of the glory of God,
-Romans 3:23

For if you forgive other people when they sin against you, your heavenly Father will also forgive you.
-Matthew 6:14

In him we have redemption through his blood, the forgiveness of sins, in accordance with the riches of God's grace that he lavished on us. With all wisdom and understanding,
-Ephesians 1:7-8

Blessed is the one whose transgressions are forgiven, whose sins are covered.
-Psalm 32:1

"Do not judge, and you will not be judged. Do not condemn, and you will not be condemned. Forgive, and you will be forgiven
-Luke 6:37

Then Peter came to Jesus and asked, "Lord, how many times shall I forgive my brother or sister who sins against me? Up to seven times?" Jesus answered, "I tell you, not seven times, but seventy-seven times.
-Matthew 18:21-22

Do not repay anyone evil for evil. Be careful to do what is right in the eyes of everyone.
-Romans 12:17

And when you stand praying, if you hold anything against anyone, forgive them, so that your Father in heaven may forgive you your sins."
-Mark 11:25

Therefore, as God's chosen people, holy and dearly loved, clothe yourselves with compassion, kindness, humility, gentleness and patience. Bear with each other and forgive one another if any of you has a grievance against someone. Forgive as the Lord forgave you
-Colossians 3:12-13

Get rid of all bitterness, rage and anger, brawling and slander, along with every form of malice. Be kind and compassionate to one another, forgiving each other, just as in Christ God forgave you.
-Ephesians 4:31-32

Whoever claims to love God yet hates a brother or sister is a liar. For whoever does not love their brother and sister, whom they have seen, cannot love God, whom they have not seen.
-1 John 4:20

My dear brothers and sisters, take note of this: Everyone should be quick to listen, slow to speak and slow to become angry, because human anger does not produce the righteousness that God desires.
-James 1:19-20

SCRIPTURES ON COMPROMISE

"If you love me, show it by doing what I've told you.
-John 14:15 MSG

As it is, you are full of your grandiose selves. All such vaunting self-importance is evil. In fact, if you know the right thing to do and don't do it, that, for you, is evil.
-James 4:16-17 MSG

Saul died in disobedience, disobedient to GOD. He didn't obey GOD's words. Instead of praying, he went to a witch to seek guidance. Because he didn't go to GOD for help, GOD took his life and turned the kingdom over to David son of Jesse.
-1 Chronicles 10:13-14 MSG

All who indulge in a sinful life are dangerously lawless, for sin is a major disruption of God's order.
-1 John 3:4 MSG

You're cheating on God. If all you want is your own way, flirting with the world every chance you get, you end up enemies of God and his way.
-James 4:4 MSG

Calling the crowd to join his disciples, he said, "Anyone who intends to come with me has to let me lead. You're not in the driver's seat; I am. Don't run from suffering; embrace it. Follow me and I'll show you how. Self-help is no help at all. Self-sacrifice is the way, my way, to saving yourself, your true self. What good would it do to get everything you want and lose you, the real you? What could you ever trade your soul for?
-Mark 8:34-37 MSG

A person without self-control is like a house with its doors and windows knocked out.
-Proverbs 25:28 MSG

Meanwhile, the saints stand passionately patient, keeping God's commands, staying faithful to Jesus.
-Revelation 14:12 MSG

Teach me your way, Lord, that I may rely on your faithfulness; give me an undivided heart, that I may fear your name.
-Psalm 86:11

Such a person is double-minded and unstable in all they do.
-James 1:8

No one can serve two masters. Either you will hate the one and love the other, or you will be devoted to the one and despise the other. You cannot serve both God and money.
-Matthew 6:24

SCRIPTURES ON CLOSED DOORS

These are the words of him who is holy and true, who holds the key of David. What he opens no one can shut, and what he shuts no one can open. I know your deeds. See, I have placed before you an open door that no one can shut. I know that you have little strength, yet you have kept my word and have not denied my name.
-Revelation 3:7-8

"Who shut up the sea behind doors
  when it burst forth from the womb,
when I made the clouds its garment
  and wrapped it in thick darkness,
when I fixed limits for it
  and set its doors and bars in place,
when I said, 'This far you may come and no farther;
  here is where your proud waves halt'?
-Job 38:8-11

Paul and his companions traveled throughout the region of Phrygia and Galatia, having been kept by the Holy Spirit from preaching the word in the province of Asia. When they came to the border of Mysia, they tried to enter Bithynia, but the Spirit of Jesus would not allow them to.
-Acts 16:6-7

On the evening of that first day of the week, when the disciples were together, with the doors locked for fear of the Jewish leaders, Jesus came and stood among them and said, "Peace be with you!
-John 20:19

Then the man brought me back to the outer gate of the sanctuary, the one facing east, and it was shut. The LORD said to me, "This gate is to remain shut. It must not be opened; no one may enter through it. It is to remain shut because the LORD, the God of Israel, has entered through it.
-Ezekiel 44:1-2

SCRIPTURES ON OPEN DOORS

Ask and it will be given to you; seek and you will find; knock and the door will be opened to you.
-Matthew 7:7

Blessed are those who listen to me, watching daily at my doors, waiting at my doorway.
-Proverbs 8:34

I am the gate; whoever enters through me will be saved. They will come in and go out, and find pasture.
-John 10:9

Here I am! I stand at the door and knock. If anyone hears my voice and opens the door, I will come in and eat with that person, and they with me.
-Revelation 3:20

After this I looked, and there before me was a door standing open in heaven. And the voice I had first heard speaking to me like a trumpet said, "Come up here, and I will show you what must take place after this.
-Revelation 4:1

He gives strength to the weary and increases the power of the weak.
-Isaiah 40:29

for he satisfies the thirsty and fills the hungry with good things.
-Psalm 107:9

but those who hope in the LORD will renew their strength. They will soar on wings like eagles; they will run and not grow weary, they will walk and not be faint.
-Isaiah 40:31

Peace I leave with you; my peace I give you. I do not give to you as the world gives. Do not let your hearts be troubled and do not be afraid.
-John 14:27

Come to me, all you who are weary and burdened, and I will give you rest.
-Matthew 11:28

And my God will meet all your needs according to the riches of his glory in Christ Jesus.
-Philippians 4:19

The lions may grow weak and hungry, but those who seek the LORD lack no good thing.
-Psalm 34:10

If you remain in me and my words remain in you, ask whatever you wish, and it will be done for you.
-John 15:7

SCRIPTURES ON SPIRIT, SOUL, BODY

Do not be afraid of those who kill the body but cannot kill the soul. Rather, be afraid of the One who can destroy both soul and body in hell.
-Matthew 10:28

and the dust returns to the ground it came from,
and the spirit returns to God who gave it.
-Ecclesiastes 12:7

For the word of God is alive and active. Sharper than any double-edged sword, it penetrates even to dividing soul and spirit, joints and marrow; it judges the thoughts and attitudes of the heart.
-Hebrews 4:12

Then the LORD *God formed a man[a] from the dust of the ground and breathed into his nostrils the breath of life, and the man became a living being.*
-Genesis 2:7

As the body without the spirit is dead, so faith without deeds is dead.
-James 2:26

So I say, walk by the Spirit, and you will not gratify the desires of the flesh. For the flesh desires what is contrary to the Spirit, and the Spirit what is contrary to the flesh. They are in conflict with each other, so that you are not to do whatever you want.
-Galatians 5:16-17

And Mary said: "My soul glorifies the Lord
and my spirit rejoices in God my Savior,
-Luke 1:46-47

What good will it be for someone to gain the whole world, yet forfeit their soul? Or what can anyone give in exchange for their soul.
-Matthew 16:26

The person without the Spirit does not accept the things that come from the Spirit of God but considers them foolishness, and cannot understand them because they are discerned only through the Spirit.
-1 Cor 2:14

ACKNOWLEDGMENTS

Many people supported, encouraged, and assisted me on my journey and with this book. Thank you, first and foremost, to my Lord and Savior, Jesus Christ. I am in awe of how He takes an ordinary woman and reveals His story of hope to encourage others. He, alone, receives all the glory.

Thank you, again, to my man, Fred, for your patience and support. You and I have faced many doors together. We've made the choices, placed our hope in the Lord, and experienced His faithfulness and favor. I honor and thank God for you, Fred, and your constant commitment to walk through the doors placed before us.

Thank you to the ladies in our Small Group and others who continue to undergird us with your prayers and support.

Thank you to those who willingly shared your stories to encourage and offer hope to those reading our book. God knows the lives you're touching.

Thank you, Sherline Hudson and Dee Spivey (Shine Your Light Photography) for the pictures for our front cover.

Thank you, to everyone who purchased this book, for your support. In addition to investing in this book for yourself, a friend, or a family member, all proceeds from this book will support HIS Prison Ministries to reach those who are incarcerated and their families in Alabama.

And finally, thank you to my editor, Ebony Horton, for continuing to walk this book journey with me. On to our next assignment.

OTHER BOOKS BY LINDA WIMES

YOU HAVE TO BE WILLING TO DIE: DON'T BE MOVED BY WHAT YOU HEAR

"It's a cyst." "It's non-Hodgkin's Lymphoma." "She has not had adequate therapy..." "Her survival is in question. "The death sentence doctors declared for Linda Wimes when she refused chemotherapy seemed to mark her end. But God told her, "Don't be moved by what you hear," and that's what she believed. Journey with Linda in *You Have to be Willing to Die: Don't be Moved by What You Hear* to experience a courageous stance on faith. Follow her practical guidance for peace and stability in any situation. Experience real testimonies from others who dared to believe in a God who never changes. Learn the victory of being willing to die in order to live.

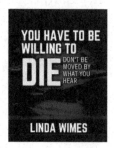

TEN SESSION STUDY GUIDE: YOU HAVE TO BE WILLING TO DIE: DON'T BE MOVED BY WHAT YOU HEAR

When doctors gave Linda Wimes a death sentence after she refused chemotherapy for an aggressive cancer, she chose instead to believe God's words to her, "Don't be moved by what you hear." In this companion study guide to Amazon Bestselling Book, *You Have to be Willing to Die: Don't be Moved by What You Hear*, Linda outlines practical guidance and reflections for you to have your own courageous stance of faith. Accompanied with personal experiences, biblical principles, and group activities, this 10-week study guide is bound to become a permanent personal reference to combat any challenge in life.

Available on Amazon and
Dove Christian Supply in Dothan, Alabama

ABOUT THE AUTHOR

Linda Wimes, just like you, has faced many doors, some of which involved life-or-death choices. Linda fully understands the difficulty of not knowing what to do when you don't know what to do. She has faced doors, not knowing whether to turn left or right, keep moving, or just give up. And in those times, Linda  continues to find hope and place her trust in the One (Jesus) who never disappoints. Linda continuously shares the message of hope to others who may need encouragement to not give up but rather to stand.

A bestselling author, Linda serves Alabama's communities in many capacities, but the position she is most proud of is Director of HIS Prison Ministries, an outreach ministry that supports those who are incarcerated and their families. Linda has spent over 35 years doing life and serving others.

Linda and her husband, Fred, have two children and live in Dothan, Alabama. She can be reached at lwimes@graceba.net